Normal 2014

Selected Works from
The First Annual
DFW Conference

Normal 2014

Selected Works from
The First Annual
DFW Conference

Edited by Emily Brutton,
Carissa Kampmeier, and Ashlie Kontos

Copyright © 2015 Lit Fest Press

Cover Image: Copyright © 2015 Chris Ayers

All rights reserved.

ISBN: 978-1-943170-05-0

Interior Design: Emily Brutton
Cover Image: Chris Ayers
Cover Design: Emily Brutton
Production Director: Jane L. Carman

Typeface: Garamond

Published by Lit Fest Press, Carman, 688 Knox Road 900 North, Gilson, Illinois 61436

festivalwriter.org

What goes on inside is just too fast and huge and all interconnected for words to do more than barely sketch the outlines of at most one tiny little part of it at any given instant—
David Foster Wallace, "Good Old Neon"

Fiction's about what it is to be a fucking human being—
David Foster Wallace, interview with Larry McCaffery

Table of Contents

Introduction   ix
   Jane L. Carman

"Strewn Along the Margins": Reading Wallace Reading   1
   Mike Miley

Reimagining Wallace   13
   Ryan M. Blanck

No One Ever Says: A Personal Reflection on Anxiety
and Addiction in Light of Wallace's *Infinite Jest*   21
   Ryan M. Blanck

Hideously Deformed and Monstrously Bulging: Pregnant Bodies
and Monstrous Reproductions in *Infinite Jest*   27
   Christine Harkin

Into the Womb of *Infinite Jest*   37
   Danielle S. Ely

Avid for All: Excisions   47
   Daniel Leonard

Weird Pretty Hand and Other Poems   53
   Francesco Levato

David Foster Wallace's Love-Hate Relationship with Consumer Capitalism *Christopher Michaelson*	59
Return to Summer *Amy L. Eggert*	73
"It takes great personal courage to let yourself appear weak": DFW on Shame, Addiction, and Healing *Ashlie M. Kontos*	81
Excerpt from "The Scissor Man" *Jeffrey Calzaloia*	93
War of the Words: *The People of Paper* and the Metafiction of Rebellion *Mark Sheridan*	99
The Ultimate "Support System": Depression, Schopenhauer's Idea of the Artist, and the Role of Art in David Foster Wallace's "The Depressed Person" *Jeff Jarot*	107
The Sheepskin Email: David Foster Wallace and Technology *Matt Bucher*	115
Hideous Absence: Contingency, Representation, and the Problems of Postmodernity *Robert Ryan*	121
Steps to Recovery: A Scattered Assembly of Tangents, Interruptions, and Asides *Diego Báez*	129
"At the Very Terminus of His Tether": David Foster Wallace and the Situationist Ghost *Z. Bart Thornton*	135
Lisa Is the Water *JoAnna Novak*	145

'Radically antifundamentalist': Notes Toward 155
a Post-Secular Poetic in David Foster Wallace
   Shannon Minifie

Exhausted Thread: A Commentary on Fiction's Progression 165
in Thomas Pynchon, John Barth, and David Foster Wallace
   Stephen Swain

Bios 175

Introduction

Jane L. Carman

> *I feel unalone—intellectually, emotionally, spiritually. I feel human and unalone and that I'm in a deep, significant conversation with another consciousness in fiction and poetry in a way that I don't with other art*—David Foster Wallace, Salon interview with Laura Miller, 1996

The First Annual David Foster Wallace Conference at Illinois State University was founded as a way to celebrate the life and works of David Foster Wallace. With the generous support of the Department of English and Chair, Chris De Santis, the first conference took place in May, 2014. As intern Shelly Kerker and I started to receive proposals, we found that the submissions were impressively varied with attendees coming from as far as Ireland, Poland, Canada, and from every corner of the US. We were also thrilled to see that DFW scholars were a diverse group of people working as lawyers, packing plant supervisors, seasoned scholars with several books, and undergraduate students, among many others. Equally impressive was the breadth and quality of the works submitted. The conference community was inclusive, enthusiastic, and supportive.

It is our hope to continue to celebrate Wallace through this anthology that includes creative and critical works and some works that blend the two genres. The critical examine Wallace's life and work; the creative express each author's take on what it means to be human. By placing these pieces side by side, the editors and I hope to provide a small sampling of the work Wallace inspired. The works included within this anthology are by no means exhaustive, rather they are meant to provide a glimpse into the varied and exciting scholarship presented at that first conference.

I would like to thank Charlie and Victoria Harris for sharing memories of David and for helping me make the connections necessary to get this conference off the ground. I would also like to thank the following interns and readers who made the first two conferences possible: Emily Brutton (2015), Paige Domantey (2014), Callie Dziurgot (2015), Alyssa Hanchar (2015), Mike Johnsen (2015), Carissa Kampmeier (2015), Shelly Kerker (2014), Eric Longfellow (2014), and Bryan Reid (2014). Without these scholars, the conferences would not have been possible.

"Strewn Along the Margins":[1]
Reading Wallace Reading

Mike Miley

This piece was originally published online by The Smart Set *in August 2014.*

I have David Foster Wallace's personal copy of Don DeLillo's novel *End Zone*. It is in my hands. It used to be his, and now it's mine, albeit temporarily and under careful supervision by credentialed professionals. It is teeth-chatteringly cold in this room and brain-fryingly hot on the street because it's July in Austin. People are baking cookies on their dashboards, and they're delicious. It will not rain until September.

I am relaying this information to you from the Reading Room of The Harry Ransom Center at the University of Texas at Austin, which in addition to housing the most powerful air conditioner in North America, houses pretty much every literary archive that you could dream of having access to, including the David Foster Wallace Archive, which, along with Wallace's manuscripts and correspondence, has about 300 books from his personal library, 250 of which contain copious annotations in Wallace's minuscule handwriting. I am actually being paid, or, more accurately, subsidized, to read his annotations.

There's documentation for this. The Andrew Mellon Foundation granted me a fellowship (and a private office) for a proposal entitled "Reading

---

[1] The title comes from a sentence in Don DeLillo's novel *Ratner's Star* that Wallace underlined: "what you have to do is either not publish or make absolutely sure your work leaves readers strewn along the margins. This not only causes literature to happen but is indispensable to your mental health as well. … This is the sane way to write if you're insanity-prone …"

Wallace Reading: David Foster Wallace's Glosses and the Aesthetic Benefits of Close Reading." While this may threaten to sound impressive, both the proposal's title and its contents are in reality complete and utter bullshit. There is nothing academic about my reasons for being here; I am in Austin always and only as a fan. Mere fandom, however, is not enough to convince your wife to allow you to leave her and your two toddlers behind in the mild climes of Los Angeles so that you can jaunt to the burning pit of Hell that is Austin during the drought of 2011 just to pore over the marginalia of a major American writer you're obsessed with. Phrasing it like that makes you sound irresponsible and selfish, but when you call yourself a Ransom Center Fellow and you flash some Mellon Foundation coin, you've got academic immunity and are more or less free from all other obligations.

If all this sounds a bit strange, let me try to contextualize this: apart from one of his sweat-soaked bandanas or used chewing tobacco, David Foster Wallace's annotations are probably about as sacred to his fans as a piece of the True Cross is to Christians. No Wallace fan could resist an opportunity, especially a subsidized opportunity, to touch the literary equivalent of a medieval holy relic.

If that analogy makes it sound like I consider myself a pilgrim, let me bring things back down to earth because the truth is far less lofty and noble: I am not a pilgrim, and my trip to Austin is no religious pilgrimage. I came to Austin as a stalker, the kind of person who ought to be the recipient of a restraining order, not a research fellowship. The fellowship faintly disguises the fact that I am here to invade David Foster Wallace's privacy, and that I took advantage of the Mellon Foundation to satisfy my personal compulsion to get as close to the inside of Wallace's literary head as I could possibly get. What I failed to anticipate during all my academic grifting was how much peering into the dark recesses of Wallace's skull would give me the howling fantods. What I wanted, I learned, was much more than I bargained for.

This realization came fast and hard the moment I opened DFW's copy of *End Zone*. I knew the DeLillo books would be juicy because DeLillo was pretty much Wallace's favorite author, but that was no preparation for the words that greeted me when I carefully opened the book's brittle paperback cover:

"SILENCE = HORROR."

My breath tripped in my throat. I was hoping for revealing annotations, and Wallace exceeded my expectations with his first gloss. Freaky things like "SILENCE = HORROR" are not the first thing a researcher stumbles across anywhere outside of a TV show. Wallace may have been talking about *End Zone*, but the context was totally different now; these were words from beyond the grave, written in a dead man's hand, and even though I'd never met him, here I was holding his treasured book, staring his mind in the face, and his first utterance to me is "SILENCE = HORROR." Wallace, the self-described "math weenie," had written the perfect equation, one that has come to represent his silence, the horror of his death, and, as I realized later, my silence, my horror. Equations, after all, work both ways. And this was only the beginning.

Three books after *End Zone*, I opened a book whose annotations chilled me deeper than the HRC Reading Room's cooling system could ever aspire to. This was the moment when I confronted the letters that have preoccupied me for the past three years and filled me with more creative fear and personal dread than I've ever felt before.

The letters appeared beside the following passage on page 87 of DeLillo's *Great Jones Street*:

> "There's nothing out there but a dull sort of horror. You can't just churn it up into your own fresh mixture. Hero, rogue and symbol that you are."
>
> "Maybe I don't want to churn it up at all. Maybe I want to make it even duller and more horrible. I don't know. One thing's sure. I can't go out there and sing pretty lyrics or striking lyrics and I can't go out there and make new and louder and more controversial sounds. I've done all that. More of that would be just what it says—more of the same. Maybe what I want is less. To become the least of what I was."

Wallace underlined that entire passage. Then he drew a line down the margin. Then he wrote these three letters: "DFW." And then he underlined them. Twice.

It's that "DFW" in the margin that haunts me.

I only thought I knew what "DFW" meant before. It was fanboy shorthand for the literary icon and hero that is David Foster Wallace, but to

Wallace, "DFW" stood for the literary entity known as David Foster Wallace, his writerly persona that existed only on the page, apart from the living-and-breathing Dave Wallace. Wallace satirizes his literary moniker-cum-identity in *The Pale King*, where he writes "once you're fixed with a certain *nom de plume*, you're more or less stuck with it, no matter how alien or pretentious it sounds to you in your everyday life" (297), but this discomfort with his full name existed long before *The Pale King*. In a postcard to Don DeLillo, Wallace explains that

> "'Foster' is my middle name, foisted on me as part of my N.d.P. by my agent in 1985—he said there was 'already a David Wallace.' I was 23 and would have called myself Seymour Butts if he'd told me to. … Seeing my full name used in print makes me feel like Lee [Harvey] O[swald] did in *Libra*—another reason that book is probably my favorite of yours …"

In this postcard, Wallace connects the inclusion of his middle name to his hunger for success and approval—the name represents a business decision, a means of standing out in the book market, a decision that was not his and that he has come to feel trapped by years later. It is an identity that he cannot escape—it's been "foisted upon" him—especially on the page. And what does this have to do with Lee Harvey Oswald? It seems like an extreme comparison, but look at page 416 of DeLillo's *Libra*:

> "It sounded extremely strange. He didn't recognize himself in the full intonation of the name. The only time he used his middle name was to write it on a form that had a space for that purpose. No one called him by that name. Now it was everywhere. He heard it coming from the walls. … It sounded odd and dumb and made up. They were talking about somebody else."

And so when Wallace came across a passage in someone else's fiction that he identified with, he wrote his initials in the margin. Most of the time, he elected to use "DFW" rather than "DW," implying that he was relating these passages to the literary persona that he felt both shackled to and alienated from.

I'm sure most of us identify with or are touched by passages in the things that we read. That is, after all, one of the reasons that we read. Some of us—diehards perhaps—may even underline them or copy them into a notebook or commit parts of them to memory. But I have never heard of anyone writing his/her initials in the margin of a book. And I've certainly never heard of someone doing all of the above and then some. This is obsession, capital-I Identification, the kind that seems excessive and bizarre because that's exactly what it is.

After finding my first "DFW," I wasn't interested in finding anything else in his books. As a Ransom Center staffer delivered each new stack of books to me, the only question I found myself asking was "will this one have a DFW in it?" I never questioned whether seeing a "DFW" might not be a good thing to see, that the presence of one on the page might mark a painful, private moment in Wallace's life, one that I had no business seeing, let alone being eager to encounter.

Wallace's initials appear twenty-one times in seventeen books, books ranging from novels to memoirs to literary anthologies to writing guides to philosophy and self-help books, and nearly every "DFW" or "DW" in Wallace's archive appears next to a passage about creating, or, more precisely, the failure to create. And the "DFW"s that don't appear alongside gut-wrenching descriptions of arrested creativity accompany withering descriptions of imbalanced, acutely self-conscious mental states, which only adds to the overall impression one gets of Wallace's mental image of himself as a solipsistic failure, a gifted person who has lost control of his gift and now lives as a prisoner to "DFW" and all of its demands, demands he fears he will never be able to fulfill.

"DFW" represented a classic Wallaceian double-bind to Wallace: it encapsulated his talent and his limitations, the force that blessed him with creative stardom and cursed him with aesthetic failure. His talent, the very thing that held the world in awe of him, was what Wallace viewed as his greatest antagonist, the elusive force that continually threatened to abandon him, leaving him mediocre, forgotten, silent, left with only the horror of failed genius.

Joseph Frank's book *Dostoevsky: The Stir of Liberation* captures this double-bind rather well. Even though Wallace was reading Frank's bio as an assignment for *The New York Times Book Review* (during his time aboard the cruise ship he would later christen the *Nadir*, no less), he still wrote "DFW" next to this passage on page 334 discussing *Notes from Underground*: "The underground man's vanity convinces him of his own superiority and he despises everyone; but since he desires such superiority to be *recognized* by others, he hates the world for its indifference and falls into self-loathing at his own humiliating dependence."

Wallace also underlined a related sentiment on page 117 of DeLillo's novel *Ratner's Star*. "The work's ultimate value was simply what it revealed about the nature of his intellect. What was at stake, in effect, was … his identity …"

And then there's this one from page 55 of Apostolos K. Doxiades' novel *Uncle Petros and Goldbach's Conjecture*: "How terrible it must have been for him, if after such a brilliant beginning he suddenly began to feel his great gift, his only strength in life, his only joy, deserting him." In the margin, Wallace wrote "DW; Self-pity; Faint :(."

In his copy of R. D. Laing's book *The Divided Self*, Wallace drew a parallel between himself and one of Laing's case studies. For one individual, Laing wrote, "the loss of an argument would jeopardize his existence," and Wallace wrote that this would be "Like DFW's loss of ability to write fiction." When Wallace sat down to write, this is what lay on the line for him. He had to be "DFW" or he was no one at all.

To give you an idea of how concerned Wallace was about being unable to live up to the image of "DFW," one of his books in the HRC library is *On Writer's Block*. That's not a typo: David Foster Wallace, author of the 600,000-word maximalist opus *Infinite Jest*, owned a book about overcoming writer's block. Several of his letters to Don DeLillo express his envy of writers like William T. Vollmann and Joyce Carol Oates, who had the ability to crank out a new novel what seemed like every six months while Wallace struggled to produce a novel each decade. These letters even pepper DeLillo with amateurish questions such as "Do you have like a daily writing routine?" And this was after he'd published *Infinite Jest*!

Wallace relays his struggle to produce work in a consistent and disciplined manner in a letter to DeLillo: "… it's frustrating to feel that I'm getting mature and more disciplined in some areas of adult life and yet still seem a slave to my moods and emotions when it comes to work." Later in the same letter, Wallace even relates the shame of how private and isolating this struggle actually is when he describes the "sad manically charming and loquacious letters" he receives "from young writers who struggle" with writer's block "and tell me that they regard me as some paragon of steady drive and discipline, which letters I try to answer politely but they make me feel fucked-up and Unknown." This feeling is perhaps best expressed in something he wrote in the margins of *On Writer's Block*: "style-self perjury nicotine trip double bind re: IJ [*Infinite Jest*]—want both to guarantee similar reaction and to avoid being repetitive, derivative of self."

Wallace's challenges with maintaining discipline as a writer caused him to experience a sense of alienation from his own prodigious talent, as these two passages in Walter Kaufmann's introduction to Richard Schacht's *Alienation* amply show:

> "The student who chooses to become a scientist or writer, painter or philosopher, is apt to feel that the competition has become so deep that it defies comparison with previous ages. … he has no assurance that he will be able to make a living in his chosen field, and there is much less reason to expect that he will ever make his mark by doing something really worthwhile. And this is one of the most crucial experiences associated with alienation."
>
> …
>
> "… the creative life is full of depressions, and very few have talent enough to find an overall sense of satisfaction in it …"

These two passages appear on the same page. Wallace underlined them both. He also wrote "DW" beside each of them. Two on the same page. Reading these annotations in the frigid HRC Reading Room filled me with the same disbelief you probably feel now. Wallace's creative angst affected his entire view of himself and his grip on reality. For instance, look at this passage from page 211 of DeLillo's *Libra*:

> "… the language tricked him with its inconsistencies. He watched sentences deteriorate, powerless to make them right. The nature of things was to be elusive. Things slipped through his perceptions. He could not get a grip on the runaway world."

Wallace underlined this and wrote "DFW" beside it.

Page after page, book after book, the annotations in Wallace's library fixate upon Wallace's deepest creative fears, fears that begin with his identity as a writer but end up questioning his existence as a human.

In "How Tracy Austin Broke My Heart," Wallace claimed that he generally found sports biographies "breathtakingly insipid" pieces of writing, but that does not appear to prevent him from finding himself revealed on page 139 of *Muscle: Confessions of an Unlikely Bodybuilder* by Samuel Wilson Fussell:

> "I who could remember every test score I'd ever received back to the second grade, yet couldn't remember half of my teacher's names. I who had cynically selected every academic institution I'd attended not for its offerings but for its reputation. I'd been far less interested in an education than in documented proof of scholarly success. Even Bamm Bamm's search for war wasn't too different from my own entry into the gym. As long as we created for ourselves a rite of passage, we could instill our lives with meaning."

He drew a line down the margin and wrote "DW" beside it. Not "DFW," the writer, but "DW," the person. He wrote the same initials beside this passage from Robert Stone's *Dog Soliders*, page 42:

> "Fear was extremely important to Converse; morally speaking it was the basis of his life. It was the medium through which he perceived his own soul, the formula through which he could confirm his own existence. I am afraid, Converse reasoned, therefore I am."

But the most devastating passage of all, the one that over time has caused me to reconsider the purpose and worth of this whole project, comes from page 307 of DeLillo's *Americana*:

> "There is no book, Davy. There's eleven pages and seven of them don't have any words on them. And I'm not making any great claims about the other four."
>
> "I thought you were writing all the time you were up in Maine. How long were you up there?"
>
> "Almost a year," he said.
>
> "What did you do all that time?"
>
> "I don't know. I really don't remember much of it. I guess I was stoned most of the time. I think I blew a fuse or something. My head went dead. That's the only way to put it. Something in there burned out and blew away. Went dead."
>
> "And you were in that garage for a whole year. And you weren't doing anything?"
>
> "I was doing something. I was killing my head."

He underlined this passage and wrote "DFW" next to it.

It does not take many interpretive leaps for one to see the parallels between this passage and events in Wallace's life: substance abuse, writer's block, self-loathing, mental breakdowns, right down to the garage-turned-writing room. Although the writer in this passage is not the one named David, the passage in this context takes on the quality of Wallace having a conversation with himself. This, it seems to me, is as close a view of Wallace's mind as you can get. This stuff is as private as private gets. The impulse we feel to avert our eyes is no accident.

I think this passage helps me to see why I balked earlier at the idea of calling my quest in Austin a pilgrimage. These annotations are not holy relics because they restore nothing. Rather, they are simply the fears and obsessions of a damaged soul laid naked on the page, pushed to the margins but hardly marginal. A close encounter does not provide more salvation.

No one ever talks about how identifying with something you read might not always be a good thing. Saying "that's like me" is not always an affirmation—it can be terrifying and make you feel "more fucked-up and Unknown." Critics and fans alike rhapsodize about identifying with David Foster Wallace's writing as though it can only be consoling and empowering, and I used to think so too, until I got too close and discovered what may be the most important truth about literature, the true "aesthetic benefit of close reading," though I doubt the Mellon Foundation would be all that interested in hearing about my discovery, as it is beneficial only in the most cautionary of senses: there is such a thing as reading too closely.

Wallace's annotations suggest that he had been reading too closely, searching for too much validation, guidance, or comfort in the books he read, to the point that his reading only wound up reinforcing his worst tendencies. Wallace found no escape from himself while he was reading; rather, his personal library remained just that: personal, continually bringing him back to his own struggles and inadequacies.

And I found myself in danger of following him. Yes, this begins and ends up being about me, the guy in the frosty reading room in Austin, for fandom is always about the fan; the self is always the subject. The artist is, at best, the mask fans wear to distract themselves from the fact that they are looking into a mirror. I learned far more about myself through reading Wallace reading than I learned about David Foster Wallace. I discovered I had been reading Wallace too closely. For years I looked to Wallace for answers to just about everything—how to think, how to live, what to read and how. Turns out, I got what I wanted, if what I wanted was a more erudite way to criticize myself or a higher, more crippling level of self-consciousness than I already had. I did wind up understanding myself better, if only to understand where I might be headed and what I must avoid becoming.

This is why I've taken over two years to finish writing this, why I've stalled out time and time again in search of the right voice or style or insight into something that feels both too large for me to take on and too close for me to see clearly. This "DFW" persona, this mental state of Wallace's, was a reflection of mine as well, albeit distorted and exaggerated through a funhouse mirror darkly. Wallace's work reads like a more articulate, insightful version of the ticker-tape running in our own skulls—this is the cliché that everyone employs to describe Wallace's writing, and for me it is absolutely true. However, no one really interrogates what that statement means or how far something like that goes. If I keep reading Wallace this closely, will I end up resembling him even more closely? Do the devices I borrow from him here—self-aware reportage, direct interrogation, hyperbolic jokes about mundane locations—show that I have moved beyond him or simply fallen further under his influence? If I continue on this path of emulation, will I reach the same conclusions about being alive as he did?

In his work *In Quest of the Ordinary*, Stanley Cavell writes "to acknowledge that I am known by what this text knows does not amount to agreeing with it … To be known by it is to find thinking in it that confronts you." Wallace wrote "DW" next to this. I must agree, and the confrontation I had with Wallace's thinking is one I fear that I'm not resilient enough to endure in the long term. What I saw went beyond fandom, beyond hero-worship, beyond sympathy—it was simply pure fear and horror. And it has often shocked me into silence.

I know Jonathan Franzen has led the lynch mob in criticizing Wallace's fans for elevating him to the status of "Saint Dave," and although the truth is important and I should be working to overcome sanitized, heroic depictions of complex human beings, I cannot live with the Wallace I saw, the private Wallace, the one Franzen's talking about. I can live with Saint Dave. It's a lie, I know, but a necessary one for me if I can ever hope to continue reading his work. Doing the work of getting to the truth about Wallace gets me too close to truths about myself that I am healthier for not obsessing over, at least if I want to live to see fifty. Not every truth ought to be lived with. Some truths must be overcome.

Among all Wallace's annotations, I found several that I would also have written my own initials next to, if I were so inclined, but doing so would be too revealing, too frightening, like saying the name of someone you're trying to forget.

But there is one I feel comfortable with, though for entirely self-serving reasons. It's from DeLillo's *Americana*, page 336:

> "David, I truly love and truly hate you. I love you because you're a beautiful thing and a good boy. You're more innocent than a field mouse and I don't believe you have any evil in you, if that's possible. And I hate you because you're sick. Illness to a certain point inspires pity. Beyond that point it becomes hateful. It becomes very much like a personal insult. One wishes to destroy the sickness by destroying the patient. You're such a loveable cliché, my love, and I do hope you've found the center of your sin ..."
>
> MM

David Foster Wallace underlined this passage. I don't know why he didn't write his initials next to it, but I know that his not doing so has made room for me to add mine. DeLillo's words give voice to my conflicted feelings about DFW, feelings that I cannot bring myself to utter in my own voice, despite the fact that their truth and intensity grow daily. I don't have the guts to speak them; I can only underline, transcribe, highlight, leaving my emotions strewn along the margins.

My unironic gratitude and admiration go to The Andrew W. Mellon Foundation Research Fellowship from the Harry Ransom Center, Flintridge Preparatory School in La Cañada, CA, and Team Miley, all of which provided support for my research.

Reimagining Wallace

Ryan M. Blanck

It all started with a trip to Barnes & Noble. My wife and I were browsing the aisles when we stumbled upon *The Brick Bible*, a graphic novel-style depiction of the biblical narrative recreated in Legos. Inspired, my wife and daughters and I started our own Lego Bible blog.

When I saw the Call for Papers for the first annual DFW conference, I thought this could be the perfect opportunity to marry two of my greatest loves: Legos and the writings of David Foster Wallace. I spent the next couple of months crafting Lego sculptures to represent some of my favorite scenes.

The pictures that follow are selections from the presentation made at the conference. I will let them speak for themselves.

"Little Expressionless Animals" : Julie and her younger brother abandoned by the side of a deserted road.

"Death is Not the End" : The Poet lounges by the pool in his completely secluded yard.

Infinite Jest: Ken Erdedy is paralyzed by the simultaneous ringing of the phone and the buzzing of the doorbell.

Infinite Jest: The Medical Attache unwittingly inserts The Entertainment video disc.

Infinite Jest: The Eschaton

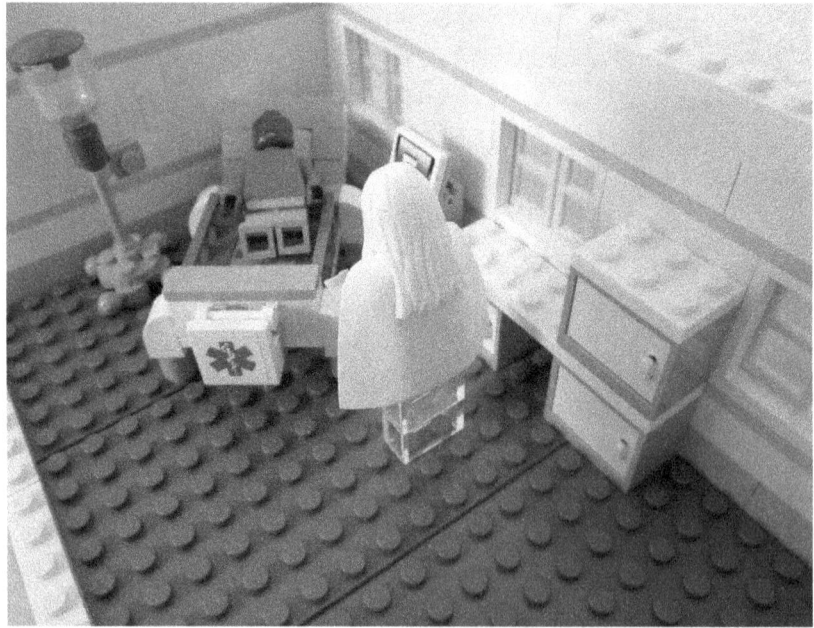

Infinite Jest: Don Gately is visited by the Wraith while he lies in a hospital bed.

"Forever Overhead" : The boy stands atop the high dive on his thirteenth birthday.

"Good People": Lane Dean, Jr. wrestles with the news of Sherry's unexpected pregnancy.

The Pale King: Chris Fogle's 'conversion experience' as he listens to the substitute accounting professor.

The Pale King: Shane Drinion levitates as he focuses on Meredith Rand's story.

"This is Water": The 'hot, consumer hell-type situation' of the end-of-the-day rush at the grocery store.

David Foster Wallace: reimagined in Lego.

No One Ever Says: A Personal Reflection on Anxiety and Addiction in Light of Wallace's *Infinite Jest*

Ryan M. Blanck

John Lennon so eloquently sang, "Life is what happens when you're busy making other plans." More often than not, "life happens" despite all my plans and preparations. Such was the case here. I planned to present one paper, life happened, and now I am presenting this paper instead. Perhaps, barring any unusual circumstances, I'll be able to present the original paper idea at a future conference.

My original presentation was to be on the topic of addiction, specifically as it relates to technology and media. I still wish to tackle the topic of addiction, but this time from a more personal angle.

In a conversation transcribed in the *NY Daily News* on May 18, 2010, Dave Moore and Bill Manville discuss two reasons why so many artists are drawn into addictive behaviors, particularly alcohol and drug abuse. First, art is borne out of strong, often negative, emotions. Many artists find illicit substances to be a means of coping and dealing with—or escaping from—those deep-seeded emotions. Second, some artists use those substances as a means of deepening their experience of those strong emotions. Drugs and alcohol can actually be the catalyst for feeling more deeply and for creating their works of art.

The list of language authors who struggled with addictions is staggeringly long: Stephen King, F Scott Fitzgerald, even our own Saint Dave, to name only a few. But these afflictions are not limited to artistic types, nor are the addictive substances limited to hard drugs and hard drinks. Instances of many media-related addictions have risen in recent years. There are the obvious ones like pornography or online shopping, but there are also less obvious ones like online gaming or social media.

The tangible world, as well as the virtual world, is full of addictive stimuli. And like the artists discussed by Moore and Manville, we find ourselves in the grip of addiction because we are either seeking an escape from our world or a means of enhancing our experience of it.

But to paraphrase what John Lennon sang, "Addictions are what sometimes happen when you're busy making other plans." No one drinks that beer or smokes that joint or logs onto the Internet with the intention of becoming addicted. We turn to these things looking for something else, only to find ourselves in the grip of addiction. And such was the case in my story…

I'm sure you remember them, all those "Partnership for a Drug-Free America" commercials from the mid-80s. They were a staple of the afterschool television diet of my entire generation. Who could ever forget those taglines?

"This is your brain. This is your brain on drugs. Any questions?"

"I learned it by watching you!"

And "No one ever says, 'I want to be a junky when I grow up.'"

These words and images were burned into my consciousness at a pretty young age, and they have proven to be quite effective. This—in addition to my extreme fear of getting into trouble—kept me away from any sort of drug, illegal or otherwise. The closest I ever got to any illicit substance as a youngster was when the kid I hung out with in middle school showed me an unsmoked joint someone had given him. None of my childhood friends ever did drugs (at least not to my knowledge). Hell, I don't think that I would've known where to find any drugs even if I wanted to try them.

I made it through my high school and college years unscathed, and continued on the straight and narrow into adulthood as well. And then, if this wasn't enough, a few years ago I crossed paths with Ken Erdedy at the beginning of *Infinite Jest* (chapter 2; pages 17-26). Ten anxiety-filled pages of reading about Erdedy waiting for an unknown woman to show up with the marijuana for his one last binge weekend. Erdedy's plan for quitting is to smoke so much pot that he makes himself so sick that he will never want to touch the stuff again.[1] I don't know if this experience is what later lands him in rehab, but it certainly worked for me. If ever I had even an ounce of desire to try marijuana or any other illicit drug, those ten pages cured me for good. If that is what the "junky" life is like, then no thank you.

30 September 2009. As I got up from the lunch table in the teachers' lounge, the room started spinning. It only lasted a fraction of a second, but what followed scared the bejesus out of me. Once back in my classroom for 5th Period, my heart rate quickly accelerated, my blood pressure shot up, and the room continued to spin while I tried to lead my sophomore English class in a discussion of Kurt Vonnegut's short story, "Harrison Bergeron." I stumbled over my words and could barely put together a coherent sentence. In a matter of minutes, I went from standing at the whiteboard to sitting on my large wooden stool to sitting at my desk, trying to avoid actually falling over altogether. I was in the middle of what I would realize later was my first real panic attack.

I told my students that I was not feeling well, so they should find something to do quietly while I sat at my desk, freaking out over what was happening to me. When the bell ending the period finally came, I bee-lined it to the nurse's office as students cleared out of my classroom. The school nurse checked my vitals, then told me to call my wife to pick me up and take me to the doctor, then sent me to lie down while I waited for her to arrive. My pulse and blood pressure were very high, but not high enough to warrant an ambulance ride to the nearest ER. About 40 minutes later, my wife showed up, I got in the passenger seat, and we were on our way home. We stopped at my doctor's office, where he gave me a pretty thorough once-over. He couldn't find anything really wrong, so he figured my symptoms were probably stress-related.[2] He said to go home and relax, take the next day off, and try some stress-management techniques to keep my stress levels down.

---

[1] David Foster Wallace, *Infinite Jest*, 22.
[2] Even though we were less than a month into the new school year, I was already having a tough time. My teaching load was very demanding, and on the home front, my family and I had been relocated to an extended-stay hotel for a couple of weeks. We had to have work done on the stairwell and landing to our second-floor condo, making our unit inaccessible. So, yeah, I was under a little more stress than normal at the time.

16 October 2009. Some two weeks after this incident, as my AP English Language class began after lunch, I once again felt like I had been swept under by a wave of dizziness. I tried to take roll, but struggled to get each name out as my heart rate and blood pressure once again skyrocketed while the room seemed to spin out of control. I could hardly make it through roll call, let alone my scheduled lesson plans in this condition,[3] so I once again told my students to take out homework to work on while I sat at my desk counting the minutes until the bell rang.

Long story short, a few hours later I found myself in urgent care in the midst of yet another panic attack, this one being far more severe than the one I had two weeks prior. While I was lying on the gurney, the doctor asked me a whole host of questions as the nurse hooked up the EKG and checked my other vitals. One question he asked me repeatedly—confidentially, of course—was whether I had used any drugs recently: cocaine, speed, anything. After his examination, he determined that either I was a closet cocaine user in the midst of an overdose or withdrawals or something, or else there was "something seriously wrong" with me.[4]

Once my vitals dropped down into the normal range, the doctor sent me to get a bunch of blood tests done; the results all came back normal that following Monday.[5] There was nothing physiologically wrong with me, so the doctor figured that my symptoms were most likely anxiety-induced. Despite the doctor's optimistic prognosis, I still felt horrible most of the time over the next several weeks (most likely anxiety-induced symptoms). Determined to get to the bottom of things, I had a long series of doctors' appointments with a variety of specialists. The neurologist was the first to put a real label on my condition and diagnosed me with "vertiginous migraines," and prescribed an anti-anxiety medication for me that is also supposed to help prevent migraines.[6] The drug was marginally successful

---

[3] In addition to a second round of these physical symptoms, I was scared out of my skull.
[4] Looking back, I've realized that that is the worst thing a doctor could tell someone in the middle of a panic attack.
[5] The doctor didn't tell me all of what he was testing for, which in hindsight was probably for the best. They were testing for some pretty scary shit, and I was already scared out of my mind. So telling me about the potentially life-threatening conditions he was testing for probably would have sent me completely over the edge.
[6] The stuff he prescribed was the one medication that a relative with anxiety issues warned me not to let my doctor put me on. Against my better judgment, I accepted the prescription anyway. I was desperate for some sort of relief and was willing to try just about anything.

at the beginning, but I saw very little real improvement over the next couple of years. For the most part, I suffered migraines almost once a week and lived in constant fear of another panic attack.

Fast-forward about three years. My employer switched insurance carriers, forcing me, once again, to switch doctors. As my new doctor reviewed medications during my initial consultation with him, he asked me about the anti-anxiety medication my previous doctor had prescribed. He said this medication was for symptomatic treatment, not for prevention. Basically, it would be like taking an aspirin for the pain of a broken arm without setting or casting the broken arm. And since this medication was essentially a sedative, he said it was likely interfering with my sleep and actually *worsening* my sleep apnea as a result; he said it was likely putting me into too deep of a sleep, so my body probably wasn't waking itself up when I stopped breathing, so my brain wasn't getting enough oxygen and my body wasn't getting enough rest. And, to top it all off, it was highly addictive.[7] In other words, I'd been taking the wrong medication for three years, and this wrong medication was most likely doing far more harm than good. My doctor then prescribed a new medication for me and told me to wean myself off the old one.

That weekend, I began the "detox" process, which would last almost a month. I tried to go off of it gradually at first, but then decided to just go cold turkey. I wanted to get it out of my system as quickly as possible rather than dragging out the process.

The first two weeks were filled with nausea, dizziness, insomnia, tremors…it was pure hell. I lost over ten pounds from not eating. I couldn't focus on my work, or anything else happening around me. I missed roughly three days of work. I slept a lot. I was stuck in a fog, disconnected from reality around me.

These initial symptoms began to subside after about two weeks; then the insomnia took over. I guess this makes sense since I had been taking a sedative every night for over three years. I had no trouble falling asleep; it was staying asleep that was difficult. I'd wake up every morning at about 4:00 a.m.—sometimes even earlier than that—and just lie there tossing

---

[7] My wife pointed out the irony that at the start of this, the doctor thought I was a drug addict based on my symptoms. But then to treat my symptoms, the doctors turned me into a drug addict.

and turning, trying not to wake up my wife until it was time to get up for work. I averaged maybe four hours of sleep each night, not nearly enough to get me through a full day of teaching. And the worst part was spending those early morning hours tossing and turning with Taylor Swift songs playing over and over and over in my head.

After the fog lifted and I was able to rejoin the land of the living, I began to reflect on this experience. I was—I *am*—a recovering drug addict. Me, Mr. Vanilla.[8] I was one of those kids who never, ever said, "I want to be a junky when I grow up." And yet, here I was on the tail end of my recovery from a three-year addiction to a prescription sedative. I am a recovering junky. Sure, mine wasn't your run-of-the-mill drug-addict story: I wasn't offered pot in the locker room. I didn't fall in with the wrong crowd in high school, nor was I pressured into trying some pills at a party. I didn't lose my house and job and family to my drug addiction. I was simply a young man desperate for relief from nearly debilitating anxiety that manifested itself in excruciating migraine headaches. And because of that desperation, I took the first pills offered to me by a neurologist who seemed to have little regard for the long-term consequences.

I never thought this would be a chapter in my white-as-Wonder-Bread story. I never imagined when I was younger that I'd be missing days of work, curled up in bed in fetal position, trying to sleep off the withdrawal symptoms of a full-blown detox. Likewise, I'm sure that in his younger years Ken Erdedy never thought he would be paralyzed by the sounds of the phone and doorbell ringing at the same time, unable to decide which one to answer for fear that the one he doesn't answer is going to be the woman bringing him his drugs. I'm sure Don Gately never thought he'd be reduced to burglary to support his drug habit, or that he'd end up the victim of a gun battle outside a halfway house. And Tiny Ewell and Kate Gompert and Randy Lenz and Poor Tony Krause. I imagine none of them planned to end up where they did. No one plans this sort of thing. No one thinks it will happen to them. No one ever says… well, you know the rest.

And yet, here they… here we are. Recovering addicts taking it one day at a time.

---

[8] I don't smoke or drink or chew, and I don't go with girls that do.

Hideously Deformed and Monstrously Bulging: Pregnant Bodies and Monstrous Reproductions in *Infinite Jest*

Christine Harkin

Author's Note: Edited for length, the following excerpt represents the second half of a paper on how pregnancies in *Infinite Jest* are used as tropes to support narrative needs, but that the text doesn't grant pregnant characters voice or agency. The paper examines Clenette as the only pregnant body given voice to narrate in the first person, and then only a single line; Mildred Bonk as a silent pregnancy referenced glancingly in Victorian-era modest manner yet juxtaposed with Lenz's murderous spree and the subsequent scene's major blood-spattering, bellowing, wince-inducing fight; Gately's mom, abused while pregnant, as first in a series of pregnancies (including the AA story of a pregnant wife waiting for groceries and Millicent Kent's sister), which serve to heighten the damage and abuse borne of addiction; C.T.'s mom, strapped to the delivery table and immobile in a narration that tells of her labor sixth-hand and in terms only of the medical staff attending her, as the pinnacle of pregnancies used as set pieces to make a point: in this case that C.T.'s story is unknowable; Mario's birth, a surprise to the narrator but potentially not to Avril, the latter not given access to the reader to tell her story.

The large excision of text that makes all these points—referencing Julia Kristeva's and Judith Butler's theories of abjection as well as feminist readings of lack of agency and embodiment—in essence argues that human pregnant bodies exist in *Infinite Jest* to heighten the stakes of addiction, to metaphorically and literally reproduce the damage of parental choices. What follows is the second half of the argument, about the geopolitical and film pregnancies in the novel. The entire paper is under submission for journal publication and is available here christine-harkin.squarespace.com/config#/pages|/wallace-paper

Mario's deformities are echoed in another pregnancy invisible to most in the novel. In *Infinite Jest*'s geopolitical dystopia, an American poisoned region of annular fecundity and toxicity is forced upon Canada: a section of the Northeastern United States is cartographically redrawn as Canadian and then subject to frequent catapulting of nuclear waste, a process Elizabeth Freudenthal calls, "a domestic drama inscribed in patriarchal terms of manifest destiny" (Anti-Interiority 199). Like the polluted womb of the freebase mother—a reproductive site interrupted by toxic substances—*Infinite Jest*'s mythic annular region in what used to be the Northeastern United States chokes off growth with toxic substances then blooms with fecundity as the waste obliterates everything and wipes the slate clean for new growth. In renaming the U.S.-Canadian-Mexican political union O.N.A.N., however, the U.S. isn't spilling its masturbatory wastes, but rather foisting them upon Canada to render that nation Abject. The resulting convexity is not so much "reconfigured" as co-opted for gestation of O.N.A.N. waste, which serves the fictional Johnny Gentle's goal of uniting Americans "in opposition to 'some cohesion-renewing Other'" (Boswell 124). For what is more abject than a maternal body gestating unwanted wastes?

Once the U.S. removes itself from this region, walling off and aiming giant fans at what is abject and Other, the debate over naming this abjection ensues. Dominant power lies with the patriarchy, but there is resistance from the impregnated state. Alain, the Canadian film scholar refers to the Convexity in a discussion of how, "filth by its nature it is a thing that is always creeping back" (233). His disdain for the filth catapulted upon his home, and implied threat that it will come back to haunt the U.S. foreshadows the resistance's efforts to punish American excesses with the deadly film known only as The Entertainment. The filth that comes creeping back is not just the nuclear waste, but consumerism, entertainment culture, and narcissism.

When his interlocutor corrects Alain's naming of the disputed region, the latter bristles. "'I meant Convexity. I know what is the thing I meant.... Convexity.'

'Con*cav*ity.'

'Con*vex*ity.'

'*Concavity* damn your eyes!'" (233). Despite this accusation of failed vision in an absence vs. bulging debate, the difference lies not in sight but in discomfort and embodiment. Identification with the bulging cartography frames each experience differently. U.S. residents, distancing themselves from the expatriated toxicity see their nation as now bereft. Missing something. Lacking. Concave. Canadians, on the other hand, feel their sovereignty has been violated and borders distended around a toxic, cyclically fertile and barren bulge. An unwanted growth. Convex.

David Hering posits an elegant reading in which he elucidates triangular ideations in the text as intentional representations of a sierpinski gasket. He argues that the reconfigured annular region "is significant thematically, as it conflates a delineated outline of a triangle with the image of a cycle" (Hering 93). But a graphic representation of the experialist area of O.N.A.N. in a map meticulously drawn by William Beutler shows a remarkably fetal shape in the area forced upon Canada by a masturbatory O.N.A.N.[1] The circular cycle, then, is represented by a maternal roundness and shape of an eight-week fetus.

---

[1] This visual, incidentally, could offer a medical argument that the Canadian pregnancy is marked by placenta previa, a dangerous condition that might be deadly for Quebec, the fetal region, or both.

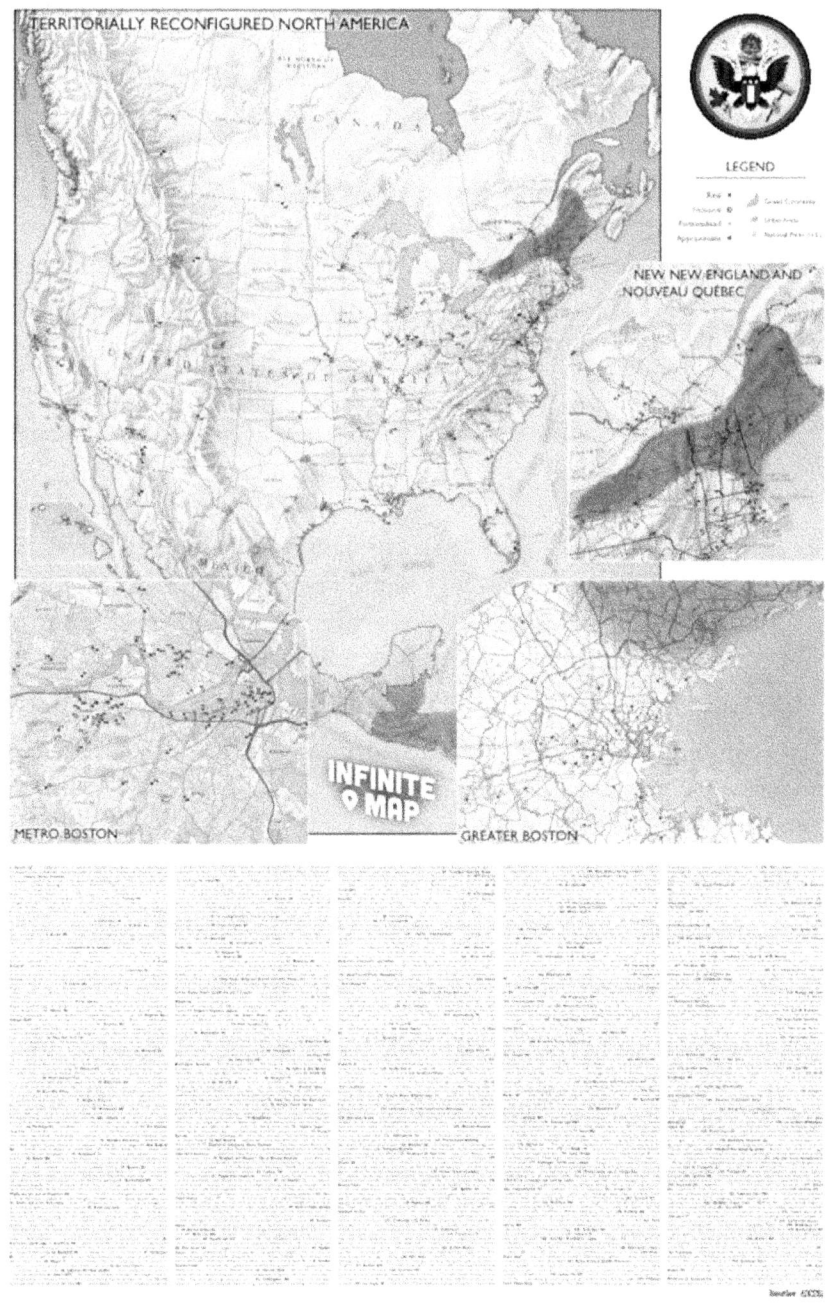

Used with permission. *Infinite Atlas* is licensed by William Beutler under a Creative Commons Attribution License.

In the folklore of post-reconfiguration North America, giant feral infants roam this disputed region between Canada and the United States, materializing the gestating waste into embodied, abandoned, damaged and toxic babies. Just before the toxic flinging began, residents fled, and rumors abound in the text about babies left behind and made supernaturally large by subsequent aerial assaults of toxic waste, and about nuclear-energized and reanimated aborted fetuses roaming the area. The typically malapropistic yrstruly relates the urban myths that within the toxic reconfigured region exist:

> infants the size of prehistoric beasts roaming the overfertilized east Concavity quadrants, leaving enormous scat-piles and keening for the abortive parents who'd left or lost them in the general geopolitical shuffle of mass migration and really fast packing, or, as some of your more Limbaugh-era-type cultists sharingly believe, originating from abortions hastily disposed of in barrels in ditches that got breached and mixed ghastly contents with other barrels that reanimated the abortive feti and brought them to a kind of repulsive oversized B-cartridge life (*IJ* 562).

The absentee patriarch of this nursery of feral infants and abortive feti, unlike Ruth van Cleve, is not reprimanded by social services. The hegemonic structures that punish postpartum women who abandon their babies do not apply to masturbatory nation-states that abandon their waste in another, now bulging, geopolitical body. Unlike the self-reborn but silent addict who sees responsibility in the dessicated stillborn, The United States seems not to notice, "what still clung by a withered cord" nor the implied "business-end of the arrow of responsibility" (374). In fact, the increasingly frequent need to catapult more waste, to reconfigure a geopolitical body with increasingly large injections of toxic substances, shows the U.S. addiction to masturbatory consumptions fully within the realm of compulsion. Freudenthal notes that this "compulsiveness is specifically gendered, an 'annular agnation'—a cyclical, exclusively male lineage—of political power" (199). Reproduction here of deadly levels of consumption aligns with the other pregnancies in the novel as caution against addiction.

The Canadian Convexity may be a polluted uterus, but unlike the other wombs in *Infinite Jest*, the Convexity is not inflicting self- and infant-harm with substances; rather, toxins are foisted upon that sovereign body by another. Shooting waste into an unwilling Canada foments moral disgust about American wasteful, selfish, narcissistic addictions, rendering the toxic region successfully abject as part of the now-deformed Other. The "U.S.A.'s Experialistic 'gift' ... constituted an intolerable blow to Canadian sovereignty, honor, and hygiene" (59), much like the textual pregnancies Nuala Finnegan reads as a violation to the mothers' sovereignty, wherein "the woman features as invaded territory sheltering the monster foetus" (1010). In such a reading, the Convexity is not only violated and hideous, but also represents the systematic geopolitical subjugation of a nation and culture that renders it impotent, lacking a voice about its own borders and physical future. Canada is forced to unwillingly reproduce the U.S.'s monstrous and wasteful narcissism, bulging with unwanted American wastes yet unable to control the gestation, termination, or birth of this hideous growth, subject to a political union that bars self-determination and choice. Canada is subject to what Hering calls "physical subjugation," and thus victim of a patriarchy that redraws Canada as a captive body, co-opted into forced reproduction. Its silence and subjugation is sacrificed to the same textual purposes as the other maternities of the novel.

In a text of passive pregnancies, Canada represents the one acknowledged convexity that vocally and violently rejects its bulge. And though Canada has no political right, because of the O.N.A.N. forced geopolitical marriage, to choose whether or not to reproduce U.S. waste, *Les Assassins des Fauteuils Rollents* seek to reclaim autonomy, agency, and bodily sovereignty for Canada.[2] The AFR, then, might be read as vigilantes for reproductive choice, cartographic intactivism, and self-determinism. The textual impetus for the Quebecois assassin endeavors rises concomitant with the monstrous fetus of Canada's Convexity: it is because of the bulge that *Infinite Jest* characters "hear the squeak" (1034) of murderous, damaged Quebecois separatists. The rise of damaged male bodies in defense of a cartographic pregnant body could be read as paternalism wherein men seek to avenge a nation raped and impregnated by a lecherous neighbor. But insisting on bodily sovereignty is an essential characteristic of humanity, not gender.

[2] "The AFR's stated aims being nothing less total than the total return of all Reconfigured territories to American administration, the cessation of all E.W.D. airborne waste displacement and ATHSCME rotary air mass displacement activity within 175 kilometers of Canadian soil, the removal of all fission/waste/fusion annulars north of the 42 N/ Parallel, and the secession of Canada *in toto* from the Organization of North American Nations" (*IJ* 1056)

More productive than this preliminary revenge narrative is a reading of the unification of damaged bodies against a common patriarchal foe. Their use of brooms in Antitoi Entertainment offers a horrifyingly grotesque unification of domestic and phallic that, for our purposes, successfully navigates the multigendered space between two biological extremes, placing the wheelchair assassins somewhere beyond gender and subverting assumptions about the relative powerlessness of atypical bodies. The AFR's concomitant resistances to gender and power norms, borne of a unity of purpose from being externally altered, locates the possibility of revolution within embodied abjection. And in this aim, pregnant bodies fulfill both Kristevan and Butlerian definitions of atypical, altered, and horrifying in the reminder of expulsion and death. The bulge becomes a site of resistance and power, so that, rather than reproducing the U.S. addictions, the Convexity pregnancy begets a new disruption of prescriptive ideologies.

The Quebecois separatists harness pregnancy rather than seeking to terminate it. They use the film *Infinite Jest* to render inarticulate and helpless its victims—to infantilize the culture that has subjugated Canada and befouled Quebec—rather than fighting to remove the "hugely convex protective walls of anodized Lucite [that] hold back the drooling and piss-colored tetragenic Concavity clouds" (92-3) to let the filth creep back (233). They fight, not to castrate the patriarch, and not to abort the growth, but to use the power of maternity to exorcise the source of Quebec's ecological catastrophe. The film-as-weapon is largely unknown to the novel's narrator, but most evidence suggests the deadly Entertainment features a pregnant-looking woman resolving heightened, Freudian mother-child issues.

People performing an intentional resistance to social injustice by holding up a mirror to a wastefully addicted nation in order to render it powerless, are the sort of revolutionary, non-gendered bodies that Butler suggests will unravel the gender binary. And the tool they use to recapture their voice, agency, and power reinvests pregnancy with the agency that few of *Infinite Jest*'s textual gestations are allowed. We know through limited and unreliable narration by Joelle van Dyne and Molly Notkin that at least part of the mortally compelling film *Infinite Jest* around which the novel's plot spirals recreates the experience of being infantile and having a still-pregnant mother apologize incessantly (940). Filmmaker James Incandenza had a wife who'd been through three pregnancies, and might therefore have been filming a pregnant-looking woman apologizing to a newborn because he knew postpartum bodies still closely resemble pregnant bodies. More likely, though, he was creating a creative space in which the implied newborn viewer, seeing a pregnant mother figure, is somehow to know that the full uterus in question is, in fact, still gestating the viewer. That the hypnotically deadly film is so compelling because it creates a liminal space in which the viewer exists as both inhabiting and wanting to reclaim its womb-home. This fantasy of returning to infancy, and, in fact, of returning to the womb, as well—being both post-birth and still gestating, external enough to see and hear mother, and yet not quite distinct— in the Lacanian pre-verbal, pre-mirror-stage, represents a wholeness that Lacan alleges all humans seek. This wholeness, then, what Boswell calls "a return to…maternal plentitude" (131), a state in which bodily and psychological damage are erased, incapacitates and infantilizes viewers, robbing them of their power by sating their desires. This is particularly important in a text wherein maternal work and needs are subsumed by the narrator, who deflects them to textual purposes. The film's maternal apology, then, mitigates the reproduced damage of toxic parental choices, and eases birth's introduction into a seriously damaged society. It gives an authorial voice to the long-silent mother, asking it to fulfill the child's needs rather than maternal needs in seeking forgiveness for, one would assume, ever letting the child enter such a dreadful world.

The weapon with which the AFR seek to terminate the U.S.'s addictive cycles uses maternal power to assuage the cruelty of birth. Fighting for the subjectivity of their mother country using the unadulterated power of a pregnant and postpartum mother, the vigilante group embraces abjection to break the hold patriarchy has over the narrative. This revolutionary use of filmic maternity to fix damaged culture further suggests that those at the top of society (white tennis academy's headmaster and auteur) and bottom of society (cult of damaged men and addicted women) work together to cease the reproduction of American waste, addictions, and paternalism.

And if maternal voice can change a fatally addicted culture, *Infinite Jest*'s "mother-death cosmology"(229) predicts that being rendered insentient and incoherent by The Entertainment's maternal apology means rebirth will proceed from the terminus of the novel undamaged and whole. Like Gately, we are lying on the beach with the tide way out, facing a new culture of our own making that transcends patterns of reproduction to beget a conscious and thoughtful society.

Works Cited

Benzon, Kiki. "'Yet Another Example of the Porousness of Certain Borders': Chaos and Realism in *Infinite Jest*." *Consider David Foster Wallace*. Ed. David Hering. Los Angeles: Sideshow Media Group P, 2010. 101-12.

Boswell, Marshall. *Understanding David Foster Wallace*. U of South Carolina P, 2004.

Finnegan, Nuala. "Reproducing the Monstrous Nation: A Note on Pregnancy and Motherhood in the Fiction of Rosario Castellanos, Brianda Domecq and Angeles Mastretta." *Modern Language Review* 96.4 (2001): 1006-1015.

Freudenthal, Elizabeth. "Anti-Interiority: Compulsiveness, Objectification, and Identity in *Infinite Jest*." *New Literary History* 41.1 (2010): 191-211. 20 May 2014.

Hering, David. "*Infinite Jest*: Triangles, Circles, Choices & Chases." *Consider David Foster Wallace*. Ed. Hering. Los Angeles: Sideshow Media Group P, 2010. 89-100.

Houser, Heather. "*Infinite Jest*'s Environmental Case for Disgust." *The Legacy of David Foster Wallace*. Eds. Konstantinou, Samual Cohen and Lee. Iowa City: Uof Iowa P, 2012. 118-142.

Lennon, Kathleen. "Feminist Perspectives on the Body." *The Stanford Encyclopedia of Philosophy*. Ed. Edward N. Zalta. Palo Alto: Plato.Stanford.edu, 2010. <http://plato.stanford.edu/archives/fall2010/entries/feminist-body/>. 16 May 2014.

Minogue, Sally, and Andrew Palmer. "Confronting the Abject: Women and Dead Babies in Modern English Fiction." *Journal of Modern Literature* 29.3 (2006): 103-125. 13 March 2014.

Wallace, David Foster. *Infinite Jest*. Boston: Little, Brown & Company, 1996.

Into the Womb of *Infinite Jest*

Danielle S. Ely

Charges of misogyny have followed Wallace's personal life and career, from being accused of simply not being able to write female characters, to being ranked #10 out of 10 on Thought Catalog's "Male Authors Ranked by How Awful They Were to Women," with the subtitle "We forgive you." However, I believe it is possible to (permanently) suspend questions of Wallace's misogyny if we look at the misogyny running rampant in his masterwork of fiction, *Infinite Jest*.

Infinite Jest Club for Men

Infinite Jest can certainly be characterized as a male centered novel. *Infinite Jest*'s three main narratives: Enfield Tennis Academy, O.N.A.N v. A.F.R, and Ennet House, for the most part, feature male characters. We do of course have a number of prominent female characters like Avril, Joelle, Kate Gompert, Luria P., and Molly Notkin. However, the time and energy spent on/in female-driven narratives is much less than the time and energy spent on/in male–driven narratives. It's true, *Infinite Jest* is "awful to women," but once we locate the source of misogyny, it becomes easier to see that it serves a function[1] within the novel—which is the kind of thing I can "forgive."

Figurants

Female characters in *Infinite Jest*, more often than not, feel like:

> Human scenery ... seen (but not heard) ... sort of human furniture. *Figurants* the wraith says they're called, these surreally mute background presences whose presence really [reveal] that the

---
[1] A topic worthy of its own study.

camera, like an eye, has a perceptual corner, a triage of who's important enough to be seen and heard v. just seen. (Wallace 835)

Even though the women of *Infinite Jest* aren't exactly "mute," I don't think they truly speak for themselves. It would seem that if the "camera" decides "who's important," then we're only able to "see and hear" what the "camera" wants us to (835). When it comes to female character's time in the spotlight there is a man behind the camera yelling cut, but it isn't Wallace. The easy question to answer is: who's the man behind the camera? The more difficult question to answer is: what does he want us to see?

The Absent Center

In "*Infinite Jest*: Too Much Fun for Anyone Mortal to Hope to Endure," from his book *Understanding David Foster Wallace*, Marshall Boswell importantly describes James O. Incandenza's deadly *Entertainment* as the novel's "absent center" (127). Though the film itself is "shrouded in mystery," Boswell assures us that the film acts as a plot device around which much of the narrative "advances or retreats," thus justifying its place at the center of the narrative (126, 127). The importance of Boswell's recognition of the film as the novel's "absent center" is that it suggests the novel has been symbolically emptied of something, yet he offers little suggestion for what that "something" may be (126). I suggest that a more troubling absence in *Infinite Jest* is anything genuinely feminine.

Blind-Spots

To be sure, there are several scholars who examine *Infinite Jest* with an eye toward gender inequality, Andrew Steven Delfino[2] and Maria Bustillos[3]

---

[2] Andrew Steven Delfino, in his Master's thesis called "Becoming the New Man in Post-PostModernist Fiction: Portrayals of Masculinities in David Foster Wallace's *Infinite Jest* and Chuck Palahnuik's [sic] *Fight Club*," examines sexual difference from a masculine point of view. Delfino questions both normative masculinity's dominance and its underlying essentialism of sexual difference. Delfino describes *Infinite Jest* as a fictional portrayal of masculinity that "does not deal with women or respond to feminism … or even the backlash against feminism in any prominent way," and so he concentrates on "what can be learned about … masculinity … from portrayals of men among men" (3).

[3] Maria Bustillos writes "Gender issues, to me, take a very distant back seat to what I see as the larger issues in the book … All this by way of saying that, while I like thinking about all kinds of perspectives w/r/t IJ ('with respect to' *Infinite Jest*), I think they could draw you away from the book's 'real concerns', maybe, if you gave them 'too much weight.'" Bustillos goes on to clarify that she believes *Infinite Jest* is not at all concerned with "gender issues," but rather with "human issues"(Bustillos, *Wallace-1*).

being primary examples. Although their work represents two different approaches to the topic of gender in *Infinite Jest*, both seek to dismiss the importance of a focus on the feminine/female characters. In an attempt to reach "the book's real concerns," Delfino and Bustillos have cast the female/feminine aside, almost as thoroughly as the book itself has (Bustillos, *Wallace-I*). Indeed, this "muted" feminine not only points to a fundamental "blind-spot" in the text itself, but in scholarly readings of it as well[4] (Grosz "ethics of alterity," 179, "sexual difference," 109).

The Entertainment as Speculum

Fortunately, Luce Irigaray is dedicated to a life-long project of unraveling "discourses which necessarily contain a repressed or unconscious 'feminine' element" (Grosz "sexual difference," 103). She writes, "The feminine has thus far functioned in muted, suppressed, or unheard ways," and the same is true of the feminine in *Infinite Jest* (Grosz "ethics of alterity," 179). Irigaray's method of investigation is uniquely qualified to accomplish this task of (re)location.

Irigaray's "deconstruction of phallocentric representations of women and female sexuality relies on psychoanalytic theory to provide both a deconstructive 'tool' and a major [target] for her criticisms" (Grosz "sexual difference," 113). As a tool of critique, Irigaray's *speculum* is able to illuminate various "points of repression (of the feminine)" which she calls "blind spots" or "residues" (Grosz "sexual difference," 109). According to Grosz, these "blind-spots/residues" indicate points where "one subjectivity (the masculine) has taken it upon itself to represent the other (the feminine) ("sexual difference," 103, 109; "ethics of alterity," 179). Certainly, Irigaray's "exploitative technique runs the risk of "reproducing an unrecognized phallocentrism" in that her "critique relies on what it criticizes" ("sexual difference," 113). However, Grosz argues that Irigaray's use of "psychoanalysis to criticize itself" is actually her best method of

---

[4] This is not true of all cases. In fact, in April and May of 2010, the representation of women in *Infinite Jest* became the subject of what one Wallace-1 listserv participant Gregory Carlisle, author of *Elegant Complexity: A Study of David Foster Wallace's Infinite Jest*, called "my favorite Wallace-l thread in a long time!" (*Wallace-1*). Another prominent voice on Wallace-1 listserv Elizabeth Freudenthal, spends a few moments in her essay "Anti-Interiority: Compulsiveness, Objectification, and Identity in *Infinite Jest*" talking about "Avril's and Joelle's O.C.D. as being ways to control their own domestic space because they are living in a man's world and cannot control any other spaces, versus Johnny Gentle, whose O.C.D. allows him to control whole continents" (*Wallace-1*).

"providing a starting point in the positive construction of other images and representations" (114).

Since both Irigaray's *speculum* and *Infinite Jest*'s *Entertainment* occupy the "exact center" of their narratives, both can be used to illuminate the rest, from their positions within "the innermost cavities" (Moi 131). Thus, *The Entertainment* will be my *speculum*, i.e. both a major "tool" for and "target of criticism" (Grosz "sexual difference," 113).

A Crib's-Eye-View

In order understand how the "perceptual eye" of James' *Entertainment* works we will begin our investigation from the point of view of the film's star, Joelle Van Dyne, perhaps better known by her stage name 'Madame Psychosis' (835). Because Joelle is the only person alive who was in *The Entertainment*, she is able to tell us how she (the female/feminine) was framed, with what kind of lens, and with what result.

The scene leading up to Joelle's suicide attempt is about all we hear of her interpretation of *The Entertainment* until she is finally picked up by the U.S.O.U.S. for interrogation regarding her involvement. After much ado, Joelle confesses to her muted interviewer[5] that, "I was in two scenes. What else is in there I do not know. In the second scene, I leaned in over the camera in the crib and simply apologized…. As in my lines were various apologies." She asserts, "I doubt [James] used it all, I strongly doubt he used it all, but there were at least twenty minutes of permutations of 'I'm sorry'" (939).

The most important thing that Joelle reveals about her role in *The Entertainment* is that she is "not exactly veiled," but "[her] face wasn't important" (940). This attests to her belief that James didn't go out of his way to make sure that she was recognized (940). In other words, Joelle didn't believe herself to be the sole subject of the film, or her beauty the reason for the film's lethality, and I don't either. She continues by saying: what "was" important was the fact that the "point of view was from the crib, yes. A crib's-eye view" with a lens fitted with "an auto-wobble" which "no doubt was supposed to reproduce an infantile visual field" (940). Clearly, Joelle represents a mother-figure and the viewer represents her child. But what is she apologizing for? Even if there is a real need for mothers to apologize

---

[5] Steeply?

to their children, wouldn't it be better if they were allowed to speak on their own behalf? *The Entertainment*'s first offense then, against a genuine representation of femininity, is that Joelle functions as a stand-in for all mothers. Even worse than this reduction, is the way that the film presupposes that the feminine has something to apologize for to begin with.

Molly Notkin

Though unreliable in its own unique ways, the testimony gleaned from Molly Notkin reiterates a lot of Joelle's own descriptions of her role as star of *The Entertainment*.

> Molly Notkin tells the U.S.O.U.S. operatives that her understanding of the [*Entertainment*] is that it features Madame Psychosis [Joelle] as some kind of maternal instantiation of the archetypal figure Death ... sitting naked, corporeally gorgeous, ravishing, hugely pregnant…her hideously deformed face either veiled or blanked out… anamorphosized into unrecognizability as any kind of face by the camera's apparently very strange and novel lens. (788)

Here we see a reiteration of Joelle's own insistence that "her face wasn't important." Indeed, the film's focus on Joelle's "naked [ness]" seems to serve the purpose of calling attention to her "hugely pregnant" belly, rather than her face. She is "gorgeous," but "corporeally," implying her beauty is external, rather than intrinsic (788). Despite the lens' dismissal of Joelle's face, it utilizes her feminine figure/body to reinforce some important message or meaning. If the film had halted its agenda here, its focus on the female body would still represent essentialist logic of sexual difference. While the film goes beyond appearances and even gives the feminine substance, the message turns out to be a kind of origin story that demonizes traditionally feminine roles, pinpoints the flaws of the feminine, and demands an apology for all of it.

Mother-Death-Cosmology

The message is as follows:

> Death is always female, and the female is always maternal. I.e. that the woman who kills you is always your next life's mother. This, which Molly Notkin said didn't make too much sense to her either, when she heard it, was the alleged substance of the Death-cosmology Madame Psychosis was supposed to deliver in

a lalating [sic] monologue to the viewer, mediated by the very special lens...that this is why mothers are so obsessively, consumingly, drivenly, and yet narcissistically loving of you, their kid: the mothers are trying frantically to make amends for a murder neither of you quite remember. (788, 789)

In truth, there are a number of female characters in *Infinite Jest* who very nearly fulfill the "mother-death-cosmology" portrayed by the film. For example, Luria P. seduces and then murders Orin. During an AA meeting, an anonymous stripper reveals she had given birth to "a still umbilically linked dead infant" yet "[carried] it around with her wherever she went, just as she imagined devoted mothers carry their babies with them wherever they go" (376-377). But just because these women 'play the part' or some parts of "mother-death-cosmology" does not make it fair, or true.

In fact, no other female character in the novel 'plays the part' best or is as close to being the sole subject of James' film, as Avril Incandenza. Many characters including Notkin, Orin, and Steeply think just that.

Avril Incandenza

After all, "Madame Psychosis had confessed to [Notkin] that the widow (Avril Incandenza) struck her as very possibly Death incarnate ... and that it [was] bizarre that it was she (Joelle)...whom the Auteur kept casting as various feminine instantiations of Death when he had the real thing right under his nose" (790). For Joelle, Avril literally embodies the role that she merely performs. However, even though Joelle hates Avril, she still does not cite her as the subject of *The Entertainment* (790). Notkin tells us that "Madame Psychosis tended to believe [the creation of the film] had represented little more than the thinly veiled cries of a man at the very terminus of his existential tether" even remarking that the "Auteur [was] extremely close to his own mother, in childhood" (789). Joelle offers no further motive for the film's creation, nor does she accuse anyone else of being the film's subject. She simply assures us that nobody in James' life, including his own mother, could have been inspiration for the content of *The Entertainment*, except for James 'Himself' (16).

The Womb of Solipsism

Though not necessarily as good as being 'brought-back-from-the-dead,' the wraith character is by all accounts the apparition of our dearly departed James Incandenza. The wraith's telepathic conversations with Gately at his hospital bedside provide one more, albeit unreliable lens through which to identify the film's true subject, if not Avril herself.

Importantly, the wraith imparts to Gately that "he spent the whole sober last ninety days of his animate life working tirelessly to contrive a medium via which he and the muted son could *simply converse*" (838). Despite Hal's "muteness" as being one of those 'is he/isn't he?' trademark mysteries of the novel, James clearly believed that he was and wanted desperately to fix him. As such, an admittedly "contrived medium" becomes "his [James'] last resort: entertainment… Something the boy would love enough to induce him to open his mouth and come *out*" (839). According to the wraith then, not only is the film capable of curing Hal, but the term *induce* also denotes an opportunity for 'rebirth,' a *tabula rasa*. But remember, there's a chance that Hal may not even need curing, let alone a new beginning. The trouble is not so much that a father wants desperately to help his son, but ultimately the lengths he goes, and the content he chooses in order to do so. The wraith explains, he wanted to:

> Make something so bloody compelling it would reverse thrust on a young self's fall into the womb of solipsism, anhedonia, death-in-life. A magically entertaining toy to dangle at the infant still somewhere alive in the boy … To bring him 'out of himself,' as they say. The womb could be used both ways. A way to say I AM SO VERY, VERY SORRY and have it heard. (839)

Note that "The *womb* of solipsism" is the direction in which Hal is "falling" (839). "Solipsism" is an over exaggerated self-interest to the point of alienation and "The *womb* of solipsism" is a place where Hal can find protection and comfort in his solace (839). The fact that James wants to direct Hal away from "solipsism" is noble, but "the *womb* of solipsism" implies that a woman is responsible for giving birth to Hal's exaggerated self interest in the first place (839). Though it's dismissive and reductive to conflate woman with her *womb*, the use of the word clearly demonstrates the real object of James' blame. I think it's easy to imagine Avril as the 'woman' being represented here and "the wraith confesses that he had, at one time, blamed the boy's mother for [Hal's] silence," but goes on to say "what good does that kind of thing do anyway?" (837-838). Indeed, however responsible she may be for Hal's issues, whether they are real or not, Avril is not the only woman demonized by the content of the film.

In the last line of the quote, the wraith states that "the *womb* could be used both ways" and suddenly we have the "womb" as representing two different things. The first "womb" refers to the feminine "womb of solipsism," which the film was created to help Hal avoid and the second "womb" is the film itself (839). In other words, the wraith has fitted Hal with an *artificial womb* via the experience of watching the film. While both *wombs* are appealing to Hal, the film is meant to be *more* appealing and to "reverse thrust on his fall into" the former (839). Thus, even while the wraith conflates woman with her womb, he paradoxically chooses the same vocabulary to describe his own, albeit *artificial* "medium" (838).

The *natural womb* of the mother is not what Hal requires; in fact, it is what led Hal astray to begin with, according to the wraith. Thus, not only is the mother-figure completely removed from the birth-process, she is associated with Hal's back-pedal, or "fall into solipsism" (839). Subsequently, woman's *womb*, one of her most precious assets and distinctive physical features, is taken from her and turned into a "magically entertaining toy to dangle at the infant" (839). However, this "toy" does not titillate Hal so much as it teases, toys and mocks the feminine, reminding the female that even her unique physical design can be taken from her to be recreated and turned artificial (839).

Though the *womb* is obviously not woman's only precious feature, *The Entertainment* hones in on it as if it were and marks it as the flaw in her design. However, the film's most egregious quality is its attempt to rectify all that is supposedly wrong with femininity by offering itself up as rightful replacement.

The Trial

Like Irigaray's *speculum*, *The Entertainment* is literally the camera/lens through which we get our most thorough, albeit unflattering observation of the feminine. Thus, the female figure becomes another "absent center" of the narrative, since to understand her means to "see and hear" her through the lens of *The Entertainment* (Boswell 126, Wallace 835). *The Entertainment*'s position at the "core of the story," its function as a primary plot device and key symbol, its potency, its mystery, its draw, its efficacy, and its reductive content all play a part in our simultaneous acknowledgment and ignorance of its misogyny (Boswell 126). Luckily, Irigaray's method of investigation calls for one final action to be taken. Where there are "points of repression" there are also "sites of a symptomatic eruption of femininity" (Grosz "sexual difference," 109). Without the feminine, *The Entertainment* wouldn't really stand for anything. While *The Entertainment* represses and debases the feminine, it also needs the feminine, which is the confusing and double-dealing nature of Irigaray's *speculum*. Most importantly, Irigaray shows us that through metaphorical and sometimes even literal probing, what was once a novel where the feminine had been cast aside is now a novel bubbling-over with femininity.

In summary, "Irigaray's strategy is not to use the rules to win (the game is in any case rigged) but to disrupt the old game in order to initiate new ones, 'jamming the theoretical machinery' in order to enable new 'tools,' inventions and knowledge to be possible" (Grosz "sexual difference," 139). Simply put, I, like Irigaray, have placed *Infinite Jest* "on trial" in hopes of expanding its meaning to include the feminine and at the very least form "new knowledge" (Grosz "sexual difference" 139).

It's true, David Foster Wallace did not often write female characters, or from the female perspective.[6] However, despite the many accusations thrown his way, I do not believe the most misogynist aspect of *Infinite Jest* is its author. Yes, *Infinite Jest* is largely a 'men's club.' Yes, there are very few female characters in the novel, but the problem isn't just quantity, its quality too. Thus, the real source of the misogyny rippling through the pages of *Infinite Jest* is the deadly *Entertainment*.

---

[6] With a few exceptions including the unnamed female interviewer in *Brief Interviews with Hideous Men*.

Works Cited

Boswell, Marshall. "*Infinite Jest*: Too Much Fun for Anyone Mortal to Hope to Endure." *Understanding David Foster Wallace*. Columbia: U of South Carolina, 2009. 116-79. Print.

Bustillos, Maria. "Re: Avril and DFW Reps of Women." *Wallace-1*. 29 Apr. 2010. Email Listserv.

Carlisle, Gregory J. "Re: Avril and DFW Reps of Women." *Wallace-1*. 23 Apr. 2010. Email Listserv.

Delfino, Andrew Steven. "Becoming the New Man in Post-PostModernist Fiction: Portrayals of Masculinities in David Foster Wallace's *Infinite Jest* and Chuck Palahnuik's [sic] *Fight Club*." *Georgia State University Digital Archive*: Georgia State University. 2007. English Theses. Paper 20.

Freudenthal, Elizabeth. "Anti-Interiority: Compulsiveness, Objectification, and Identity in *Infinite Jest*." *New Literary History*. 41.1 (Winter 2010): 191-211.

Grosz, Elizabeth. "Luce Irigaray and sexual difference." *Sexual Subversions: Three French Feminists*. Sydney: Allen & Unwin, 1989. 100-39. Print.

—. "Luce Irigaray and the ethics of alterity." *Sexual Subversions: Three French Feminists*. Sydney: Allen & Unwin, 1989. 140-83. Print.

"Male Authors Ranked By How Awful They Were To Women." *Thought Catalog*. 31 August 2011. Web. 3 March 2015.

Moi, Toril. "Feminist, Female, Feminine." *The Feminist Reader: Essays in Gender and the Politics of Literary Criticism*. Ed. Catherine Belsey and Jane Moore. Malden: Blackwell, 1989. 117-132. Print.

Wallace, David Foster. *Infinite Jest: A Novel*. Boston: Little, Brown and Company, 1996. Print.

Avid for All: Excisions

Daniel Leonard

this audience does not want someone else

    retained from Infinite Jest *pp.368-369*

It's another conundrum,
literally makes no sense.
Him dying.

The applause
unclenching this man
painfully full,

trying to face
somebody real, fixing
something down,

a moment, just a moment.
The head finally gave up
and went away,

ended, removed.
Everyone with confusion,
their one truth.

{Brief Men}

> *retained from* Brief Interviews with Hideous Men *p.222*

During my labor of holding the world
I am attempting to envision passion—

Me good and time light for days in a row.
Devoted to the atemporal, the motion of humanity.

A different performer assumed the role in the end,
My inconsistency that would fail and was a different man.

And me great also there.

a Hall of mind

> *retained from* Both Flesh and Not *pp.220-221*

At the grand entrance
alongside nothing, the mystery,
me [*sic*] well and in place, the *supra*,
differences oddly also one.

Its locale nameless, like dreams.

I was human in translation,
in fractions. But the outcome
was once again whole, suddenly itself.

The long-sought answer is fictional,
made-up in the plot's math
but never specified or explained.

THE COURSE OF the man

> *retained from* Girl with Curious Hair *p.275*

D.L. says it's been disorienting,
needs this man saying, working.

The answer is not in the offing.
What's fine slightly less fine.

Where is the next, the rising,
his healthy tongue.

hard resources

> *retained from* Infinite Jest *p.1055*

A Master
thanks to the hope
of suspected but
unknown love
that springs eternal,
active and alert.

Master of special value
like a loved one's,
chaos starting to emerge
as unabsorbable
mentally, emotionally.

Absorbing you, you
with footprints to fill.

His original sights,
that infallible headache
that throbs with his heart,
trying to find some
new resource for him
to inhabit everything,
something.

such as us

> *retained from* Oblivion *p.118*

It appeared to come out of nowhere.
He had been required to pull
in some complicated way.

His being was sensitive and bright.

For him the narrative appeared difficult,
he had missed himself in it.

DAVID FOSTER WALLACE

> *retained from* The Pale King *pp.232-233*

Entering an obvious paradox,
I was deeply affected.

Yesterday's hero
Gingerly got up and left
Without any sound at all.

He'd been able to read
Today's world,
To shape each given slice,
To imagine making sense
Of American images.

He went well cared for,
Held aloft.

around you, a way

> *retained from* A Supposedly Fun Thing I'll Never Do Again *p.92*

You live in time,
but it's hard to feel
your living.

A whole involves
some interval—
the *fact* yields everything.

What's Special
is to love
real life.

We come to stand
close—
all beautiful.

THE BROOM OF was

> *retained from* The Broom of the System *pp.75-76*

The bridge turned out to have only one side.
I went from being to being nothing at all.

I cannot think, much less tell.
My knowledge did not go elsewhere.

I remain a human exhibit surrounded by voices,
thoroughly transparent, special and hilarious.

I would change. We would laugh together,
sad, and hang on through the dark places.

Weird Pretty Hand and Other Poems

Francesco Levato

Weird Pretty Hand

Something called gimbal came to mind,   his picture in a glass case,

     the edge of a downed tree in the shallows

   half hidden by the bank.

      This is the way of people,

        open them up and spill their guts, or deny it and pretend they're off—

steel whistle, white gloves,   some trying to run,

               a moving lace, distended and crosshatched.

The repayment clock had started running,

I could feel the vibrationless *thip* of meat connecting,

the look on his face as his posture became acquiescent.

       He passed away last Tuesday,   but nobody noticed.

His only real friends were the damaged, the last-picked,

   collections of anaerobic men who used terms like 'strategic utilization template'

   and 'revenue vector'   in place of two hearted, and hypocrite.

Axes were involved,

  complex patterns of callus on her fingers,

  all the while watching as the woman worked her blade

  past flannel plains and canted rust,

    to the place beyond the windbreak,

     where untilled fields simmer: shattercane, lamb's-quarter,

cutgrass, and sawbrier—

  Neither said a word for the first half hour,

  just a small shrieking sound on every second pass.

The Fact of Having a Body

The whole thing felt a near fatality,
        a hexagram of cement, the sound of dry things snapping,
the corrugate trailer where he left his family—
                all the myriad little changes and rearrangements,
        the power of attention and what you pay attention to,
           a staggering girl, something that floated above with a painted face.

Imagine laughing about the attacks, or the fear,
or trying to come up to somebody and explain what was going on.

        There's something interesting about civics and selfishness,
and we get to ride the crest of it.

Fucking on the Brockengespenst

She had been eight when the body was lost

       and it lay now supine and unknowing in the weeds while its head lived on;

the whole thing a cyclone of logistical complexities,

a strange problem in developmental wiring,

                            more a parallel world,

    both connected to and independent of this one,

       operating under its own physics and imperatives of cause.

Portions of the body impacted the iron bars of a built-in ladder protruding from the west wall,

there were fires in the hills, the smoke of which hung and stank of salt,

    she sat rocking   with knees bunched up and scratched at herself

essaying to ruin the face's plan—

                    past a certain point, the element of choice gets lost

these small, identity-obscuring changes and temporal rearrangements,

    not meant to be decoded or read so much as merely acquiesced to

as part of the cost of our doing business together.

These poems were originally published by The Found Poetry Review.

Note: These poems are based on chance operations that use *The Pale King*, by David Foster Wallace, as source text. Language from the source text is collected via procedure, then reworked to shape the final poems.

David Foster Wallace's Love-Hate Relationship with Consumer Capitalism[1,2]

Christopher Michaelson

1. This is Consumption

Conspicuous consumption is as integral to the world of David Foster Wallace as water is to the life of a fish. However, just as the fish fail to notice the water all around them in the tale that frames "This is Water," conspicuous consumption occurs inconspicuously among Wallace's characters, real and imagined, who consume automatically without examination of their lives. This includes consumption of media: An addictively entertaining film in *Infinite Jest* renders viewers oblivious to their biological needs, and a cable channel finds a market for misery on "The Suffering Channel." Food is especially ripe for over-consumption: revelers boil lobsters alive without considering the objects of their salivation in "Consider the Lobster," focus group subjects digest sugary snacks in a "herdlike manner" (23) in "Mister Squishy," fairgoers eat burritos as big as their heads in "Getting Away from Already Being Pretty Much Away from It All," and Wallace himself partakes of a seemingly bottomless basket of fruit in "A Supposedly Fun Thing I'll Never Do Again." Sex, too: The hideous men of the *Brief Interviews* are probably roaming the porn convention in "Big Red Son," overindulging in the marketing of sex as though it were the real thing.

---

[1] An earlier draft of this paper was presented at the First Annual David Foster Wallace Conference in Normal, Illinois, in 2014, under the title, "Business in the Work and World of David Foster Wallace." Part of that longer paper is this paper, written for a literary audience, and the other part of that paper has been adapted for a management audience under the original title.

[2] The author would like to thank audiences at the 2014 May Meaning Meeting and First Annual David Foster Wallace Conference for their encouragement and feedback.

While Wallace's treatment of human over-consumption is often funny, he is ultimately serious about the temptations of commerce and the "unbearably sad" ("Fun Thing," 261) and debilitating effects, not only on consumers but also on workers who are passive agents of production. Like the average person, Wallace—with his propensity to binge on television, and his characters' tendency to binge on entertainment—found much to love among the offerings of consumer capitalism. That is precisely why he dreaded too much of a good thing. Two interconnected themes about consumer capitalism emerge from Wallace's writing: One is the ubiquity of commercial forces and has primarily to do with the consumer who is subject to and ultimately acquiesces to them. The other is the unexamined life of the producer who promotes these forces and in doing so sacrifices identity and meaning. This paper puts some of Wallace's commercially-oriented works from multiple genres into correspondence with business, economics, management, and marketing theory about consumer capitalism.

Why should literature scholars and Wallace aficionados care about these theories? Even if he did not intend to evoke formal scholarship, Wallace was a student of philosophical and literary theory and believed that theoretical grounding was one mark of the serious, not merely entertaining, writer (Max, 2012). The resonance of his work with theories of which he may not even have been formally aware lends credence to his vivid depictions of the problems with consumer capitalism and implores us, as he did in "This is Water," to live consciously so as not to fall victim to inconspicuously conspicuous consumption and production.

2. Ubiquitous Consumerism

In "Democracy and Commerce at the U.S. Open," consumer marketing is omnipresent, from "pointillist-neon ads for EVIAN" (129)—which, it would be unfortunate not to point out after the fish story, is bottled water—to there being a market for just about everything whether or not it is officially for sale, including scalped tickets (144), pot (157), and even DFW's own press pass (159). Even the U.S. Open itself, whose name cannot appear in a formal capacity without its trademark "a U.S.T.A. [United States Tennis Association] event" accompaniment (127), in its "relentless self-promotion" (135) sports on its grounds an ad for itself (138). Customers at the U.S. Open can no more escape the inexorable march of advertisements than a fish can escape water. Scoreboards flash ads when scores are not in play, and the eye cannot look in any direction without encountering a corporate logo. Whereas Wallace lamented in "Water" that people do not take time to reflect on the obvious things around them, at the U.S. Open (which, by the way, I should remark is one of my favorite events to attend) people are not allowed the downtime from market messaging to reflect. The ubiquity of commercialism is age-old, as he notes when he blames the Peloponnesian War on commerce.

To a keen, reflective eye like Wallace's, this relentless barrage of promotion, product placement, and persuasion becomes raw material for imparting sarcasm that begets wisdom, in the form of awareness of the manipulative forces acting upon us. To most of the target consumers of this barrage, however, it is merely so much water that goes unnoticed even as it determines their very behaviors and consumption patterns. Its ubiquity becomes a negative force when it cultivates too much of a good (or bad) thing: namely, consumption and the production necessary to sustain that consumption (or vice versa in a vicious circle). It might be overly grandiose to suggest that Wallace, in these passages, is formulating an economic theory, but it is not an exaggeration to suggest that his work raises fundamental questions, debated by economic theorists, about the endgame of capitalism: Must it grow ad infinitum? Growth is often taken as a necessity by politicians in a world in which one billion or more still live in extreme poverty (Sachs, 2005), but even a burgeoning global middle class will not moderate the allure of extreme wealth (Piketty, 2014). Necessity aside, some economists have expressed concern about the future possibility of growth amid resource scarcity (Krautkraemer, 2005). As for democracy, others have described the social destructiveness of uneven wealth creation that leaves those outside the upper classes both disadvantaged and unsatisfied (Frank, 2011).

Is consumption essential to growth? Ironically, one of the perceived impediments to China's continued economic growth is its citizens' cultural proclivity to save. The theory is that, whereas for the first few decades of Chinese capitalism's boom, increased productivity served Western consumption, Chinese producers need home-grown consumers to purchase more of their products in order to sustain equilibrium of supply and demand (Qu, 2014). In other words, the Chinese economy needs to Americanize for its growth to sustain projections. Although Wallace had little directly to say about emerging markets—in fact, he traveled relatively little outside the United States (Max, 2012), and he died before the global recession had raised serious doubts about everlasting American economic preeminence—he was worldly enough to recognize the insidious effect of American consumption habits on the global appetite and that political antipathy to the United States was in no small part a function of economic resentment. As he observes in "The View from Mrs. Thompson's," an essay about experiencing 9/11 from the Midwest, "whatever America the men in those planes hated so much was far more my America [implying consumer-driven America]...than it was these ladies'" (141).

This observation in turn raises the question, do people control the economic system or does the system control them (Sabel and Zeitlen, 1985)? Wallace's answer to this question challenges the neoliberal logic that suggests that the economic system is governed by an invisible hand that human beings are powerless to influence individually. Wallace does not trust the invisible hand alone to bring about social well-being; the sad world that he depicts is the product of market forces. Although ethicists more often blame large enterprises for the insidious effects of consumption on social and environmental well-being, Wallace does not despair of the individual's opportunity to rise above the water level to see and resist these forces. Living consciously is Wallace's simple but profound answer to what human beings should do about it.

More specifically, Wallace thinks living consciously can mitigate consumerism in two guises. In the management and marketing literature, consumerism as it emerged just as Wallace was entering boyhood sought to protect consumers against the ubiquity of and other abuses of consumer products manufacturers and marketers. Well-known management theorist Peter Drucker offered a definition of "Consumerism in Marketing" in 1969, pointing out the diverging interests between consumer and manufacturer: "Consumerism means that the consumer looks upon the manufacturer as somebody who is interested but who really does not know what the consumer's realities are." And so Buskirk and Roth (1970) assert that the presence of consumerism means the failure of marketing, since marketing is supposed to align the manufacturer's long-term interests with service to the customer's wants and needs, and consumerism is a protest against the failure to achieve product safety and suitability. Unsafe or unsuitable products led to consumerist movements, a kind of organized bargaining power of the populous, sometimes in collaboration with governments and non-governmental organizations (Weiss 1967) against the perceived abuses of manufacturers and marketers that emerged every thirty-odd years in the United States from 1900 through the 1960s, according to Herrmann (1970), and arguably emerged again in the very 1990s, the early years of Wallace's writing career.

Around the time that consumerism of the first sort was being documented by researchers, awareness of consumerism of another sort began to emerge with increasing environmental concerns brought on by dangerous chemicals and industrial failures. In this second sense, consumerism refers to over-consumption, which became a more urgent phenomenon during the years that Wallace's writing career flourished, as businesses groped for a solution to the conundrum of how to make and sell more products while also not using up scarce resources. E.F. Schumacher's *Small is Beautiful* (1973) was an early statement about the failure of producers to recognize that they were using up natural capital at an unsustainable rate. "Responsible consumption," in reference to the developing "ecological crisis," was a phrase that began to be used (Fisk 1974). In the current century, awareness of excessive emissions of greenhouse gases (GhGs) brought on by over-consumption has been propelled by reports from NGO environmentalists such as the Intergovernmental Panel on Climate Change (2007), economists such as Sir Nicholas Stern (2007), and business alliances such as the World Business Council on Sustainable Development (2010). Even as businesses increasingly realize that the "bottom of the pyramid" presents a business opportunity (Prahalad 2006), and the global middle class swells (Sachs 2005), these forces create new consumers exacerbating the problem of over-consumption. In response, green environmental messaging has come into vogue (Kronrod et al. 2012), creating confusion among consumers between what information is genuine and what is "greenwashing" (Esty and Winston 2006) and leading in some cases to sustainability being a "liability" (Luchs et al. 2010). As in the first definition of consumerism, marketing is supposed to support economic efficiency (Sirgy et al. 2012), though ethical questions have been raised as to whether marketing takes advantage of the "perpetually fooled" (Wible 2011).

Wallace's ethical concerns about the ubiquity of consumption had more to do with individual lives than with the tension between economic expansion and planetary survival, but putting his work into correspondence with the work of scholars yields a potentially richer sensitivity to how an institutional culture of excess and entertainment demeans human lives. Wallace famously referred to IJ as "a failed entertainment" and insisted on its more than 1,000-page length because he thought it important for his readers to work for the novel's payoff (Burn, 2012). Instead, the society which he depicted therein, like the society in which he lived, was riven by the ubiquitous forces of commercial marketing that yielded passive, unconscious consumption that was bad for consumers, bad for society, or both.

3. Meaningless Production

If consumers are induced by the objects of production to over-consume, producers are induced by the material rewards of consumption to over-produce. It is not always that business seeks sinisterly to promote excessive consumption; it is rather that business cannot help but do so. Business and its marketing of itself is inherently manipulative, dehumanizing consumers.

At the same time, the mandate to manipulate dehumanizes the producers who are unwittingly complicit in this scheme to promote over-consumption. Often, the perpetrators of manipulation are just doing their jobs, unaware that the "absolute voice of death" ("Water," 71) with which the cashier wishes the customer a nice day, or the "Professional Smile" ("Fun Thing," 289) with which the ship's crew greets passengers, have, like the consumers' responses, become automatic and therefore imbued with no meaningful sentiment. In "Fun Thing," Wallace entertains romantic fantasies about the steward, Petra, who cleans his cabin and replenishes his supply of fruit, but the cheerful appearance of her work, like that of the mechanics hidden below the ship's deck whose activities are strictly enforced by stern supervisors, conceals its repetitive drudgery – much as Van Maanen's (1990) anthropological account of Disney's "Happiest Place on Earth," revealed that employees are taught to be "on stage" whenever a guest is present to preserve an image of happiness.

One of Adam Smith's concerns about division of labor was that a specialist whose sole responsibility is to repeat the same process over and over again might become an efficient machine who either grows desperately bored or loses all sense of meaning, thereby resulting in a worker rendered by work to be "as stupid and ignorant as it is possible for a human creature to become" (1776/1993: 429). Concern for the plight of the bored worker is not exactly the same concern for alienated laborers (Marx 1844/1997) who are overworked and underpaid. However, as Wallace would show later in *The Pale King*, which is about boredom in a public sector workplace, the indignities of meaningless work can be as lethal as abusive work to the human spirit over time. In the parlance of political theory and business ethics, "meaningful work" can refer in the negative to conditions of work in which "workers are in effect paid for blindly pursuing ends that others have chosen, by means they [the others] judge adequate" (Schwartz 1982: 635), or it can refer in the positive to the pursuit of a calling, work that is "fulfilling" and "socially useful" (Wrzesniewski et al. 1997)

In "Mister Squishy," the practiced manipulation by marketers of their focus group subjects is at an extreme, except the marketers seem as unaware of their own deception as are their subjects. A facilitator, Schmidt, manipulates blood-sugar levels in order to elicit the desired response; his gaze automatically pans across the audience to give the impression of speaking individually to each participant; he smiles (like the "Water" cashier and the "Fun Thing" crew) without meaning it, although "[h]is smile had a slight wincing quality" (4). Even the product being tested has a name, Felonies!®, intended to appeal to the health-conscious consumer's underlying desire to consume too many unhealthy products. Wallace makes a show of Schmidt making a show of his facility with Dry Erase marker tricks, spinning them in his hand (15) and flinging them along the whiteboard tray (21). Perhaps Wallace's interest in things written upon whiteboards was that of an author contrasting his own permanent marks on the page with the erasable marks of Schmidt's ultimately pointless enterprise (Michaelson, 2015). Schmidt's purpose in this sterile office is reduced to games with utensils and focus group subjects. In fleeting moments of reflection before a mirror, he seems to recognize that his identity has been reduced to the product he has been paid to promote, seeing his own face merge with that of Mister Squishy (Michaelson 2015). Wallace's concern with workplace despair was not confined to the private sector; the Incandenza boys' father who founded the Enfield Tennis Academy microwaves his own head, and the boring despair within *The Pale King* is in the IRS (Michaelson, forthcoming), but businesspersons are not exempt from the epidemic of meaninglessness in modern workplaces. Life in the cubicled world that Wallace satires is often unsatisfying, as the narrator of "Good

Old Neon" discovers when "at only twenty-nine I'd made creative associate, and…was a fair-haired boy on the fast track but wasn't happy at all" (142). Job dissatisfaction and absence of meaning can harm health (Watson 2012), creating stressfulness (Brennan and Vinter 2012) and leading to unhappiness (Gann 2012).

Research on work motivation may seek to determine ways in which to influence external work conditions in such a way as to promote motivation internal to the worker. Vroom's (1965) Expectancy Theory of work and motivation is grounded in psychological theories of pleasure orientation and pain avoidance, positing work motivation as a function of the individual effort a worker is inclined to exert in order to achieve performance outcomes that in turn are the basis for rewards. Motivational force is supported by a reliable linkage between these factors and undermined when, for example, effort does not lead to expected performance outcomes and/or good outcomes do not lead to anticipated rewards. Vroom's work has spawned a generation of researchers studying how to get more out of workers who may otherwise have reasons to want to do or be something or somewhere other than work, and in response, research about how workers can get more out of work. For example, there is research on the centrality of work to one's life (Harpaz and Fu 2002) and on well-being in various walks of life, including work (Campbell, Converse, and Rodgers 1976). Research about work includes job characteristics theory, which seeks to study the value of features of the work itself (Fried and Ferris 1987), and research on work orientations, which examines the preferences and inclinations of the worker (Wrzesniewski et al. 1997). The moral problem with work motivation theory is that too often it positions the producer as management's object of manipulation through material reward (Michaelson 2005), much as the consumer is the marketer's object of manipulation through entertainment.

Wallace, who as a writer and person was acutely aware of the potential emotional and physical pain that professional disappointment could entail, was attuned to the motivational force of pain avoidance but was as intensely cynical about the pleasure motive. In "Fun Thing" and "Water," he expresses discomfort with the idea that hedonic pleasure should ever be the focus of a weeklong cruise, much less everyday experience. The implication that Wallace might resist, that effort might be only an instrument for extrinsic rewards, is also challenged by researchers who study intrinsic value theory, the idea that there are some things that are their own reward (Audi 2005; Walsh 1994). Studying why we do what we do by seeking to understand what work means in human lives, Pratt and Ashforth (2003) distinguish between "meaning at work"—the important but extrinsic factors that employers can try to adjust to make work more pleasant, such as camaraderie and work-life flexibility—and "meaning in work," the intrinsic reasons work might matter at all. Wallace's close-up and unorthodox perspective on these phenomena awakens the reader's consciousness to what is actually happening, by pointing out what the reader would otherwise fail to notice as so much water. The producers in Wallace's narratives seem trapped between acquiescing to the comparatively easy and unconscious impulse to consume the very entertainment they have been conscripted to produce, and searching consciously to find the meaningful existence of which that entertainment, and the workaday production thereof, deprives them.

4. Conscious Consumption and Production

In both his portraits of consumers and producers, Wallace depicts the tragic comedy of living the unexamined life, pursuing ephemeral pleasures at the expense of meaning. As he terms it in "Water," living life "unconsciously" could lead to tasteless and banal phenomena, from dancing the Electric Slide to playing Bingo to endless pampering to listening to reggae elevator music ("Fun Thing," 256-8), a cruise ship echoing the grocery store Muzak of "Water" with a Caribbean accent. These portraits involve consumer choices about what to do and producers providing a supply of meaningless products and services to satisfy demand without resulting in real satisfaction. Wallace's answer to the unexamined life was for both the consumer and producer, locked in a vicious circle of entertainment consumption and reward for production, to live consciously—to transform the vicious circle into a virtuous circle in which consumers made conscious choices about what to consume and producers made moral choices about what to produce.

For Wallace and his audience, the world of consumer capitalism appears to be a distinctly uncomfortable place. Wallace immersed himself in it because he had the rare ability to see through the water that engulfed the society in which he lived and about which he wrote. That there are researchers concerned about and seeking to make progress on the very concerns Wallace expressed—to address the culture of capitalism, consumer welfare, sustainable consumption, well-being and motivation of workers, and meaning and meaningfulness—offers hope that the problems he acutely described and responded to with laughing despair might not be so desperate after all.

Works Cited/Works Consulted

Audi, R. 2005. Intrinsic value and meaningful life. *Philosophical Papers* 34(3): 331-355.

Brennan, L., and Vinter, P. 2012. How work boredom is the new stress… and it affects everyone from office workers to those on the Afghan front line. *Daily Mail*, 2 May (cites scholarly work of S. Mann and M. de Rond).

Burn, S.J. 2012. *Conversations with David Foster Wallace*. Jackson: University Press of Mississippi.

Buskirk, R.H., and Roth, J.T. 1970. Consumerism: An interpretation. *Journal of Marketing* 34: 61-65.

Campbell, A., Converse, P., and Rodgers, W. 1976. *The Quality of American Life: Perceptions, Evaluations, and Satisfactions*. New York: Russell Sage.

Care, N. 1984. Career choice. *Ethics* 94: 283-302.

Drucker, P. 1969. Consumerism in marketing. New York: Speech to the National Association of Manufacturers, April.

Esty, D.C., and Winston, A.S. 2006. *Green to Gold: How Smart Companies use Environmental Strategy to Innovate, Create Value, and Build Competitive Advantage*. New Haven: Yale University Press.

Fisk, G. 1974. *Marketing and the Ecological Crisis*. New York: Harper & Row.

Frank, R.H. 2011. *The Darwin Economy: Liberty, Competition, and the Common Good*. Princeton, NJ: Princeton University Press.

Freeman, R.E. 1984. *Strategic Management: A Stakeholder Approach*. New York: Cambridge University Press.

Fried, Y., and Ferris, G. R. 1987. The validity of the job characteristics model: A review and meta-analysis. *Personnel Psychology* 40: 287-322.

Gann, C. 2012. Boredom, constant cheer, cynicism, and other job hazards. ABC News blog, accessed 10 November 2012 at http://abcnews.go.com/blogs/health/2012/01/12/boredom-constant-cheer-cynicism-and-other-job-hazards/.

Grant, A.M. 2007. Relational job design and the motivation to make a prosocial difference. Academy of Management Review 32(2): 393-417.

Harpaz, I., and Fu, X. 2002. The structure of the meaning of work: A relative stability amidst change. *Human Relations* 55(6): 639-667.

Hunt, S.D., and Vitell, S. 1986. A general theory of marketing ethics. *Journal of Macromarketing* 6: 5-16.

Intergovernmental Panel on Climate Change (IPCC). 2007. *Climate Change 2007: Synthesis Report.* Accessed January 2008. http://www.ipcc.ch/pdf/assessment-report/ar4/syr/ar4_syr.pdf.

Krautkraemer, J.A. 2005. Economics of natural resource scarcity: The state of the debate. Resources for the Future discussion paper, retrieved 27 July 2014 from http://www.rff.org/Documents/RFF-DP-05-14.pdf.

Kronrod, A., Grinstein, A., and Wathieu, L. 2012. Go green! Should environmental messaging be so assertive? *Journal of Marketing* 76: 95-102.

Luchs, M.G., Naylor, R.W., Irwin, J.R., and Raghunathan, R. 2010. The sustainability liability: Potential negative effects of ethicality on product preference. *Journal of Marketing* 74: 18-31.

Marx, K. 1844/1997. Alienated labor. In Easton, L.D. and Guddat, K.H. (eds.), *Writings of the Young Marx on Philosophy and Society.* Indianapolis, IN: Hackett Publishing.

Max, D.T. 2012. *Every Love Story is a Ghost Story: A Life of David Foster Wallace.* New York: Viking.

Michaelson, C. (Forthcoming). Accounting for meaning: On §22 of David Foster Wallace's 'The Pale King'. *Critical Perspectives on Accounting.*

Michaelson, C. 2015. Business in the work and world of David Foster Wallace. Working paper.

Michaelson, C. 2005. Meaningful motivation for work motivation theory. *Academy of Management Review* 30(2): 235-238.

Piketty, T. 2014. *Capital in the 21st Century* (trans. A. Goldhammer). Cambridge, Massachusetts: Harvard University Press.

Prahalad, C.K. 2006. *The Fortune at the Bottom of the Pyramid: Eradicating Poverty Through Profits.* Upper Saddle River, NJ: Prentice-Hall.

Pratt, M.G., and Ashforth, B. E. 2003. Fostering meaningfulness in working and at work. In K. Cameron, J. E. Dutton, and R. E. Quinn (eds.), *Positive Organizational Scholarship: Foundations of a New Discipline*: 308-327. San Francisco: Berrett-Koehler.

Qu, H. 2014. China's dangerous obsession. HSBC Global Connections whitepaper, retrieved 22 July 2014 from https://globalconnections.hsbc.com/us/en/articles/chinas-dangerous-obsession?utm_source=outbrain&utm_medium=click&utm_content=1&utm_campaign=global+gc+2014.

Sabel, C., and Zeitlin, J. 1985. Historical alternatives to mass production: Politics, markets, and technology in nineteenth-century industrialization. *Past and Present* 108: 133-176.

Sachs, Jeffrey. 2005. *The End of Poverty: Economic Possibilities for Our Time.* New York: Penguin.

Schumacher, E.F. 1973. *Small is Beautiful: Economics as if People Mattered.* New York: Random House.

Schwartz, A. 1982. Meaningful work. *Ethics* 92(4): 634-646.

Sirgy, M.J., Yu, G.B., Lee, D.J., Wei, S., and Huang, M.W. 2012. Does marketing activity contribute to society's well-being? The role of economic efficiency. *Journal of Business Ethics* 107: 91-102.

Smith, A. 1776/1993. *An Inquiry into the Nature and Causes of the Wealth of Nations* (ed. Kathryn Sutherland). Oxford, England, UK: Oxford University Press.

Stern, Sir Nicholas. 2007. *The Economics of Climate Change: The Stern Review.* Cambridge, UK: Cambridge University Press.

Van Maanen, J. 1990. The smile factory: Work at Disneyland. In P.J. Frost et al. (eds.), *Reframing Organizational Culture.* London: Sage.

Vroom, V.H. 1965. *Work and Motivation.* New York: John Wiley & Sons.

Wallace, David Foster. 1995/1998. A supposedly fun thing I'll never do again. In *A Supposedly Fun Thing I'll Never Do Again: Essays and Arguments.* London: Abacus.

Wallace, David Foster. 1999. *Brief Interviews with Hideous Men.* New York: Little, Brown.

Wallace, David Foster. 1998/2006. Big red son. In *Consider the Lobster and Other Essays.* New York: Little, Brown.

Wallace, David Foster. 2004/2006. Consider the lobster. In *Consider the Lobster and Other Essays.* New York: Little, Brown.

Wallace, David Foster. 1996/2013. Democracy and commerce at the U.S. Open. In *Both Flesh and Not: Essays.* New York: Back Bay Books.

Wallace, David Foster. 1993/1998. Getting away from already pretty much being away from it all. In *A Supposedly Fun Thing I'll Never Do Again: Essays and Arguments.* London: Abacus.

Wallace, David Foster. 2005. Good old neon. In *Oblivion: Stories.* New York: Back Bay Books.

Wallace, David Foster. 1996. *Infinite Jest.* Boston: Back Bay Books.

Wallace, David Foster. 2005. Mister Squishy. In *Oblivion: Stories.* New York: Back Bay Books.

Wallace, David Foster. 2011. *The Pale King*. New York: Little, Brown.
Wallace, David Foster. 2005. The Suffering Channel. In *Oblivion: Stories*. New York: Back Bay Books.
Wallace, David Foster. 2005/2009. *This is Water*. New York: Little, Brown.
Wallace, David Foster. 2001/2006. The view from Mrs. Thompson's. In *Consider the Lobster and Other Essays*. New York: Little, Brown.
Walsh, A.J. 1994. Meaningful work as a distributive good. *Southern Journal of Philosophy* 32(2): 233-250.
Watson, L. 2012. One in four office workers is "chronically bored", putting their health at risk. *Daily Mail*, 12 January (cites scholarly research by S. Mann).
Weiss, E.B. 1967. *A Critique of Consumerism*. New York: Doyle Dane Bernbach.
Wible, A. 2011. It's all on sale: Marketing ethics and the perpetually fooled. *Journal of Business Ethics* 99: 17-21.
World Business Council on Sustainable Development. 2010. *Vision 2050: The New Agenda for Business*. Accessed January 2014. http://www.wbcsd.org/WEB/PROJECTS/BZROLE/VISION2050-FULLREPORT_FINAL.PDF.
Wrzesniewski, A., McCauley, C., Rozin, P., and Schwartz, B. 1997. Jobs, careers, and callings: People's relations to their work. *Journal of Research in Personality* 31: 21-33.

Return to Summer

Amy L. Eggert

Arriving home, I find myself in an unfamiliar place; everything has changed. What I remember to be a pair of ponds divided by a slow two-lane residential overpass is now a set of parking lots flanking a four-lane, high-speed route between shopping centers and office buildings. A bike path I remember snaking through the forest preserve now veers in a different direction, away from the trees. The used bookstore where I traded lemonade stand earnings for bargain paperbacks is now an organic foods market holding outdoor rummage sales on Saturday mornings. The cul-de-sac across the street is a vacant, browning lot where a man wearing leather stares at nothing and smokes his cigarettes.

The mailbox at the curb of our property that I remember encircled by tangles of hostas and daffodils is now affixed to the side of the house by the front door, a black metallic envelope that clangs open and shut. And of course the in-ground pool in the backyard, too-blue water shimmering white under sunlight, now filled in with crushed rock and sand and dirt and topsoil, and still nothing grows there.

Even the weather seems somehow changed; the warm summer sky of fragrant breezes through screens has given way to the harsh light of a slate gray sky, a stagnant sort of mildew smell in the air, and it's June.

I agreed to stay with my parents for a few weeks, an indeterminate amount of time, however long was necessary to move Granddad into an assisted living facility, to organize and clean his house, to paint it and get it on the market, to find and insure that his end-of-life documents are in order and properly prepared for the inevitable—not because I know how to deal with these kinds of things, but because I was willing, and because my parents are overwhelmed with the process.

Hanging up with my mother that evening in April after we'd made the decision—she'd started to cry, out of exhaustion, gratitude—I couldn't help but resent my brother for not helping out with any of this, for leaving it to me to ease their anxieties, to stamp out any familial fires that sparked to life.

But I knew it wasn't fair to resent him; after all, I offered to help. This was my decision. And in the weeks leading up to the visit of unstipulated duration, I struggled not to think of my brother at all, even though the more I resisted, the more I conjured up those thoughts, and to think of summer at all was to think of my brother and vice versa, and I couldn't shake the image of his lazy, impassive gaze as the rest of us around him smoldered into a frenzied panic. So I alternated between resentment and guilt over that resentment, and I wanted so badly for him to know how angry and abandoned I felt but not to tell him.

I want to feel nostalgic as I pull into the driveway, past the place where the mailbox and the hostas and the daffodils were once rooted. I think about my brother soaping the hood of our father's sedan with a dripping sponge, gray water streaming into the street. I push the thought away, can't feel that tug of reminiscence, of longing for what was. Instead I feel a numb tingling in my fingers, a pang of paranoia as I climb from my car and the man across the street flicks a cigarette away, lights another one and stares, a fluttering dread at finding the mailbox affixed to the side of the house.

"So much to do," my mother hugs me, says, instead of saying hello. And right away we're sorting through papers and she's telling me about the intake meeting at the assisted living facility that did not go well, and she's directing my father to carry my bags back to my old bedroom, "unless you'd rather stay in Brian's room," she says, and I say my old bedroom is fine.

This is how I end up lying in my old twin bed, between sheets as old as me, and I watch the ceiling while my parents sleep, frantic trapezoids of light darting across the room as passing headlights refract through the smeared windowpane.

Granddad is my only surviving grandparent. The other three died before I was old enough to mourn the loss of them, though I recognized grief caused by their deaths in those around me. When her own mother died, my mother retreated to her station wagon in the dark garage, sat in the driver's seat with the windows rolled up, and played a Patsy Cline cassette for hours every day until the tape wore out. She didn't speak or sing along or cry, just stared straight ahead through the windshield at the frayed lawn chairs dangling from nails on the garage wall. Some days my brother and I would climb into the back seat and listen with her.

When my father's parents died in a bus accident, my father pitched our rotary phone into the kitchen window—receiver, cradle, and all—shattering the glass. If not for the cord that tethered it to the kitchen wall, I imagine we'd have had to fish the phone out of the swimming pool in the backyard. Then he sank to the floor and wept.

As we drive toward the assisted living apartment complex, my mother warns me not to bring up Granddad's house or the repairs we've been orchestrating. "He's devastated," she tells me. "And he wants to go home. Seems not to hear me when I tell him he has to stay put." My father clears his throat from the backseat. She goes on, "It's hard to blame him; he doesn't fit in there, you know. His mind is still there, but his body's failing him. We couldn't just leave him in that big house all alone to fall down those stairs or slip in the shower, or what if there was a fire? What would he do if there was a fire?"

"We did the right thing, Mom." I watch houses slide past my window.

"It's just so sad to see him feeling like an outsider. It's like when your dad and I first started going to group. Everyone tried to sympathize with our situation, but, it wasn't the same. We didn't lose our child, so it was different—"

"Like hell it was," my father snaps.

"No, honey, it was. It was different…"

I squirm under my seatbelt. To change the subject, I ask about the mailbox, why the switch, mention how the green and yellow at the curb always let me know I was coming home. "What mailbox?" My mother swerves to avoid a squirrel in the road.

Granddad watches a muted soap opera from a plastic-covered chair. His walker lies shoved onto its side by his feet, looking like a snubbed pet. "Dad, look who's here to see your new apartment." He ignores my mother as she squeezes his shoulders from behind. I crouch to his side, kiss his cheek, say, "Hi, Granddad," which collects his attention. "Hello, sweetheart," and he takes my face in both of his wrinkled and shaking palms. "Are you here to take me home?"

At night I watch the spastic patches of light scurry across the ceiling. Thoughts crowd around me, and I'm frightened by their bulk, by the way they chase and crash into each other without any space or breath or punctuation between. My brother cupping his hands over mine, careful not to release the captured, flashing firefly. Granddad's trembling touch. My father's gravid silence from the backseat. I try to push the thoughts away, but they keep accumulating, stacks of cardboard boxes of childhood things packed and too many to be stashed away. A loud pop springs me away, up from my old twin bed and toward the window that faces traffic. The cars that creep past move with an underwater quality through the smeared pane, like they're pushing through undercurrents. I have to remind myself that this is not the city where I've been living for the past twelve years. Every abrupt blast is not a gunshot. In this suburbia-turned-shoptopia, strange noises afterhours were most likely cars backfiring, raccoons toppling garbage cans, kids rocketing fireworks into the night sky from cul-de-sacs and empty parking lots. I remember scanning our street in both directions, nodding the go-ahead to my brother who lit the short fuse with our father's Zippo before we both bounded up our driveway, spinning around in time to watch pink sparks explode. I push the thought away, lie back down in bed, try not to think of my brother, watch the light on the ceiling.

Without thinking about it, I pick at paint dried on my fingernails.

Between coats, my mother meets with a lawyer about some of Granddad's paperwork, and I pick up some lunch and drive to where the fishponds used to be. At my parents' house, I know my father is watering the oval dead spot in the yard that was an in-ground pool where nothing will grow. I know his jaw is locked in a scowl as he spreads more grass seed, as he jets more hose water over barren earth. I know that he lets the nozzle slip through his fingers to land on the ground, water spilling into the dirt, that he lets it lie there, a puddle spreading away from him. I know this because when I stopped there to deliver a sandwich, I saw him through the window. I left his lunch on the kitchen table and drove away, toward this place I remember that no longer exists.

Traffic zooms past in both directions, drivers impatient, honking at each other. I choose a bench at the edge of a parking lot that was a pond, and I toss scraps of crust onto the asphalt where I used to feed ducks.

Back at Granddad's, we pull paint brushes out of the freezer, a trick my mother picked up from some home and garden television program, and get back to work. She sweeps a second coat of white onto the living room wall, and I tape off the trim in the adjoining kitchen. Drop-cloths drape furniture we've crowded into the middle of the room, sofas and lamps, jutting end tables. We walk on paint-spattered bedsheets, some I recognize as having belonged to Brian as a child, firetrucks and surf boards in primary colors.

Out of nowhere, she asks me if I've gone to see my brother recently. I change the subject, ask her to pass me a new roll of masking tape. "You've got time off; you should visit him." A renewed current of resentment followed by guilt washes over me, and I will the emotions away, the ever-ebbing tide.

"Brian doesn't care if I visit him," I say, disliking the slight whine in my voice. She hands me a wrapped roll of tape, looks at me. Her paint roller drizzles white onto a yellow surf board.

"Honey, that's not true." I avoid her gaze, tear open the plastic and scratch at the tape, spinning the roll in my hands, searching for the cut edge.

For two weeks, every morning, I've been following dirt tracks into the woods, hoping to find remnants of the old bike path, but the trails always lead back out of the trees, back to the blacktop which leads away from the forest, away from underbrush and thick tree trunks that must have always been there, and I just can't remember where we used to ride, Brian and me racing, flying on our bicycles, air and sharp branches tearing at our windbreakers, our arms, the sky over our heads lost in leaves, our legs pumping, pedaling so fast we couldn't stop even if we wanted to, which we never did.

We get a phone call from the assisted living facility. Granddad is having some sort of episode, they say, and could one of us drive over to help calm him down. I volunteer; I convince my parents to let me go alone since he still seems to bear a grudge toward them for having left him there.

When I reach his apartment, I find two nurses in scrubs keeping their distance from him, hands raised in front of their chests as though to show they bear no weapons and intend him no harm. Granddad has stripped down to a bleached pair of boxers and clutches his walker with one knotted fist. His other hand jabs a gnarled finger in accusation at the women, and he is shouting.

"Bring me my clothes! I want my goddamn clothes!"

The women speak in soothing tones, taking turns, assuring him that they haven't got his clothes. But he shouts on.

I hurry to him, position myself between his walker and the women so that he has to focus on me. "Granddad? Granddad, what's wrong? Where are your clothes? What's going on?" His cheeks, I see, are damp with tears. His naked chest, skeletal and pale, heaves with each angry breath. "Granddad, where are your clothes?" But his eyes lurch away from mine, and he glares at the nurses standing behind me. I spin to face them. "Where are his clothes?"

One of the women leads me into his bedroom, to his dresser where one drawer juts askew, a handful of socks a heap on the floor, a pair of pants crumpled in the corner. I pull open a second drawer, find it full, pull open another, find it, too, is packed with clothes. I grab an undershirt, find the tag at the neck where my mother has printed Granddad's initials with a marker. I carry it to him, hold it up for him to see. I struggle to keep my voice calm. "These are yours." He snatches the shirt from me and flings it to the floor.

"My clothes are at home. I want my clothes! I want to go home!" Again, he's glaring at the women across the room, and I have to adjust my stance to block them from his view.

"Granddad, I want you to listen to me." I take his face in my hands, the same way he held mine on my first day back in town, and I find his eyes. "This, this place is home now." He clutches his walker. His shoulders sag a bit. "This is home now."

I'm afraid he's going to fall because his knees buckle and he wilts forward, and one of the nurses steps up to help me guide him to the plastic-covered chair in front of the television set. And I think of chlorinated water splashing. A reckless teenaged dare. My granddad's hands are shaking, and I think of Brian shaking, his lips bruising blue. And one of the nurses fills a glass with tap water and slides it into Granddad's fingers and urges him to drink, drink it down, and I push my brother from my mind, but still he bobs to the surface, lifeless but alive, and I think of his deadpan gaze and his inability to talk or to tie his own shoelaces. And Granddad lets the glass slip from his fingers like my father let the hose slip to the grassless ground, and it shatters on hardwood like chlorinated water splashing like a phone smashing a windowpane like a skull on the side of a pool, and he cries and grabs onto my hand, and we're shaking, both of us are shaking. And he pulls me closer to him, and he whispers into my face, "This isn't home, sweetheart. This isn't home."

"It takes great personal courage to let yourself appear weak": DFW on Shame, Addiction, and Healing

Ashlie M. Kontos

"We are the most in-debt, obese, addicted, and medicated adult cohort in U.S. history" (Brown TED).

"So it turns out I'm not so different from you, Dad. I, too, carry a void inside—nothing exotic, just an ordinary human despair-fear-anxiety factor—and mine will try to feed on anything that gives me an instant sense of self-definition, purpose, or worth" (Maté 231).

These statements were published in 2010 and 2011, respectively, by well-established authors on shame and addiction. Their research was published over fourteen years after David Foster Wallace's predictive *Infinite Jest*. Yet Wallace was not a licensed social worker qualitatively documenting shame and addiction, like Brené Brown, nor was he a doctor observing patients on skid-row, like Gabor Maté. Wallace was a writer and an intuitively brilliant man who suffered from his own depression while witnessing U.S. culture drift into this complacent, self-numbing state. *IJ*'s depiction of addiction and recovery strikes to the root of the individual's and society's malady: shame, fear, solipsism, an existential inertia. Wallace's foresight into what would ail the emerging U.S. generations, and one could argue most of the Western world, would not be proven and understood fully by science until years later. Shame-research has flourished within the twenty-first century and been discussed in academic circles from the expected field of social work to the slightly more atypical disciplines of literary studies and neurobiological research, meaning that shame is such a permeating experience that scholars from opposing ends of the university spectrum have made an effort to understand it. Wallace's personal knowledge of addiction, its causes, and its consequences reflects what researchers are beginning to understand as an issue of society at large, not simply an isolated problem of the addict. The addict–though in a more harmful environment and state of mind–reflects society's own inner turmoil that is easily ignored and pacified via our materialistic, consumer-driven culture. Wallace recognized, "Everybody is *identical* in their secret unspoken belief that way deep down they are different from everyone else" (*my emphasis IJ* 205). Though society perceives itself as better than or distinct from the addict, it is not. Wallace's fiction and scholar's findings suggest human beings share more identical attributes than dissimilar ones; therefore, society suffers the same *DIS-EASE* as the addicts we ostracize. Wallace's fiction encourages vulnerability and authenticity–traits that help addicts overcome their struggle with substances–and almost ironically, these behaviors push the literary community out of the postmodern refrain of disillusionment, cynicism, and irony, which Wallace admittedly strove to overcome.

"He wept in shame and pain" (304),

"Marathe wondered why the presence of Americans could always make him feel vaguely ashamed after sayings things he believed in" (318),

"In other words you hide your hiding. And you do this out of shame" (535),

"I longed to be able to lean into my mother's arms and weep and confess all. I could not. For the shame" (IJ 813).

IJ abounds with individuals' shame–the desire to speak about their shame and the overwhelming fear of doing so. Shame prevents them from connecting to others; consequently, it is the birthplace of their isolation. Brené Brown defines shame as an, "intensely painful feeling or experience of believing we are flawed and therefore unworthy of acceptance and belonging" (30). *IJ* depicts addicts who all struggle with a sense of unworthiness yet yearn for connection. Lenz portrays this double-bind when he stresses over his friendship with Green; Lenz feels "this slight hangnail of fear, like clinging, whenever he likes somebody," and worries "where do you look with your eyes when you tell somebody you like them and mean what you say?…You can't go around giving that kind of thing of yourself away" (554). Lenz does not know how to be vulnerable with another person. To temper feelings of fear and shame, addicts find relief from their suffering through drugs, yet their addiction intensifies their alienation. Maté writes about this destructive cycle and asserts, "Isolation is in the very nature of addiction. Psychological isolation tips people into addiction in the first place" (102). Addicts are caught in a suffering-continuum: isolation perpetuated by shame leads to the drug, which does temporarily relieve negative feelings, but the drug further divorces the addict from others as she becomes more and more dependent on it for comfort.

Before discussing how Wallace negotiates addiction and healing in his novel, I would first like to define addiction. Vincent Felitti, MD, delineates addiction as, "an understandable, unconscious, compulsive use of psychoactive materials[1] in response to abnormal prior life experience, most of which are concealed by *shame*, secrecy, and social taboo" (*my emphasis* 9). Felitti finds addiction is such an obstacle for those who have experienced abnormal experiences because the drug provides "chemical relief from the ongoing effects of old trauma" (8). Maté similarly reports that what the addict really yearns for is not the drug, per se, but "the absence of the craving state," so the underlying problem is not the drug itself, it is the emotional pain the drug is soothing (114). The Department of Preventive Medicine Kaiser Permanent Medical Care Program reports that unrecognized Adverse Childhood Experiences[2] (ACE) "are a major, if not the major, determinant of who turns to psychoactive materials and becomes 'addicted'" because such experiences cause, "neurodevelopmental and emotional damage" in the child (Felitti 8). Neurodevelopmental and emotional damage is explained more thoroughly by Dube, SR, et al.: "Children and adolescents, who are exposed to the types of childhood experiences that we examined may have feelings of helplessness, chaos, and impermanence and may have problems self-regulating affective states. Thus, illicit drug use may serve as an avenue to escape or dissociate from the immediate emotional pain, anxiety, and anger" (586). All of the characters suffering with an addiction in *IJ* experience these emotions, and as Wallace reveals each character's past, the reader begins to understand each character has suffered some kind of adverse childhood experience.

---

[1] The Department of Preventive Medicine Kaiser Permanente Medical Care Program began by observing food-addiction–overeating and obesity–in the 1980s; they expanded their addiction observations in their 2004 report to include smoking (nicotine), alcoholism, and the injection of illegal drugs.

[2] ACE as researched by the Kaiser Program were limited to: recurrent and severe physical abuse; recurrent and severe emotional abuse; contact sexual abuse; growing up in a household with an alcoholic or drug-user; a family member being imprisoned; a mentally ill, chronically depressed, or institutionalized family member; the mother being treated violently; and/or both biological parents *not* being present (4).

Addiction takes many forms and can be found across racial, ethnic, social, and religious divides. Sex-addiction, food-addiction, nicotine-addiction, shopping-addiction, gambling-addiction, these are now common-place in the U.S. Though these dependencies are not as radical as drug addiction, they are no less harmful and enslaving to the user and the user's familial/social circle. Seemingly responsible citizens addicted to sex or shopping self-medicate their emotional suffering when they engage with their drug-of-choice; sex or shopping soothes some part of the individual that fears their needs have not, are not, or will not be met. So the citizen-addict and the drug-addict suffer from the same *DIS-EASE*. Despite the similarities between these types of addicts, society judges, imprisons, or rejects the drug-addict, while some of our own addictions go undetected or are even encouraged in our present culture (i.e. workaholism). Maté recalls his conversation with Ralph[3]—whom Maté describes as a "God-starved, pseudo-Nazi poet"—in which Ralph challenges the illusory distinction between the responsible-citizen and addict; he says:

> You collected a hundred shekels of gold [...] But what are you looking for? What have you spent your whole day searching for? That same bit of freedom or satisfaction that I want; we just get it differently. What's everybody chasing all the money for if not to get them something that will make them feel good for a while or make them feel they're free? How are they freer than I am?[4] (263-264).

Society is "freer" in that most of our functioning addictions do not lead to psychological collapse or incarceration, yet proper emotional/psychological/mental treatments for drug-addicts are less favored and ill-funded compared to incarceration. Moreover, U.S. society largely discourages and denies the self-reflection and emotional dialogue necessary to address painful experiences that lead to any kind of addiction.

---

[3] Ralph describes himself to Maté as a "schizo-affective, obsessive-compulsive, hyperactive paranoid delusional depressive with bipolar tendencies superimposed on antisocial personality disorder, and I also suffer from hallucinatory states triggered by drugs," but despite Ralph's mental/emotional instability, Maté recognizes that Ralph is one of the most intellectually gifted people he has ever encountered (77-78).

[4] Of course the claim could be made that the addict is using a substance that produces long-term harm to himself/others and contributes nothing to society, and while the corporate, capitalistic Western world may not be the beacon of ethics or health, at least that part of society contributes to Progress. Maté argues that this may not be the case because he attributes certain maladies of modernity as stemming from capitalism. He believes addiction is a product of a capitalistic society. See "Capitalism Makes us Crazy: Dr. Gabor Maté on Illness & Addiction" from *Making Contact: Radio Stories and Voice To Take Action* www.radioproject.org.

One of the reasons society neglects such self- and social-reflection is because, as Brown observes, society is "constantly overwhelmed with feelings of fear, blame and disconnection. This creates an 'us and them' world," but she concludes, "We are 'those people.'…we are the others" (Brown 145). Garrick Harden and Marcus Aldredge adopt Erving Goffman's theory of interactive rituals and discern that the "overwhelming consistency of potential embarrassment and constant guard necessary in shielding oneself, inevitably reflects a larger cultural pattern of anxiety," thus society restrains genuine emotional exchanges, which breeds emotional constriction (6). Pia Mellody's psychological research affirms Goffman's sociological theory; she discusses the effects of an emotionally disengaged culture and finds that contemporary U.S. society acts as though, "It's not ok to have feelings. That if you are a mature, well-controlled adult person who is successful, you stay out of your feeling-reality at all times and stay up in your head" (n. pag). She goes on to state, "We are taught in our culture that it is absolutely ok to medicate pain and to remove it into not feeling it," and though we all experience shame on some level, "we are not to talk about it, and we're to distort and hide it" (n. pag.). In this way, the addict and citizen are the same: they have painful emotions and try to soothe these experiences via external sources, but society rejects the addict and resists the introspection required for healing and change.

Throughout *IJ*, it is the ability to shift one's paradigm that enables the addict to change. The recovery process centers on taking responsibility for one's actions; before this can occur, the addict has to consciously choose to adopt a new perspective. Kevin Griffin, co-founder of the Buddhist Recovery Network, affirms that everyone feels an inner-hunger consequently, "addiction wasn't something outside the normal human behavior, it was just…a continuum of craving and attachment that in this sort of middle zone, we call it normal. And then when you get out to more the edges of that continuum, we call that addiction" (n. pag.). In order to get outside the suffering-continuum, addicts must choose to return to the middle zone of "normal" attachments. Wallace understands awareness to be the defining factor in how the individual chooses. For him, "'Learning how to think' really means learning how to exercise some control over how and what you think. It means being conscious and aware enough to choose what you pay attention to and to choose how you construct meaning from experience" (*This Is Water* 53-54). Gately presents the best example of how an addict reprograms his attachments, and he does so in the supportive environment of the Ennet house and AA meetings. Yet, assistance from the community and 12-step programs only Works If You Work It;

after all, seven out of ten AA members relapse (Denzin 355). As much effort that was once put into hustling for drugs and catching the next high, must also be put into the restructuring the addict's lifestyle. This must be a conscious choice enacted every day, over and over again.

As the addict claims responsibility for herself, she learns to reinvest in authenticity. This is stressed in AA with steps 4, 5, and 8-10. Hepworth, Rooney, and Lawson define authenticity as "the sharing of self by relating in a natural, sincere, spontaneous, open and genuine manner… Practitioners' verbalizations are also congruent with their actual feelings and thoughts" (120). The ease and trust needed for authentic interactions must be learned and practiced because the postmodern culture does not advocate vulnerable exchanges. Brown finds that shame prevents authenticity because "we cannot share ourselves with others when we see ourselves as flawed and unworthy of connection. It's impossible to be 'real' when we are ashamed of who we are or what we believe" (242). She states that individuals only transcend shame and embrace their authentic self via empathy and defines empathy as "the skill or ability to tap into our own experiences and connect with an experience someone is relating to us" (33). Wallace employs the White Flag Group meetings as the site in which authentic interactions incite empathy; here, "Everybody in the audience is aiming for total empathy with the speaker…Empathy…is called Identification" (345). This group cultivates empathy by being, "disgustingly humble, kind…nonjudgmental…sanguine tolerant, attentive, truthful…the only people who end up able to hang for serious time in AA are the ones who willingly try *to be* these things" (*my emphasis* 357). This genuine interaction is not a simulacrum of good behavior; it is a practiced lifestyle that requires, "attention, and awareness, and discipline, and effort" (*This Is Water* 120). Gately observes that this authenticity is not forced by The White Flag Group, "It isn't like the Group makes them do it…It's all optional; do it or die" (357). Because the postmodern culture struggles with authenticity, the recovering addict needs a group, like AA, that respects and cultivates it, making the group imperative to the individual addict's struggle.

Wallace depicts Ennet House as a place where "people are crying and making noise and getting less unhappy," a place where authentic emotional expression is understood and embraced (591). Gately recalls the wisdom 'Ferocious Frank' shared with him when he broke down and ponders, "If [Geoffrey] Day ever gets lucky and breaks down…Gately'll get to tell Day the same thing": "Ask For Help and like Turn It Over, the loss and pain, to Keep Coming, show up, pray, Ask For Help" (273). The AA culture grounds itself in such rituals as sharing one's story and reciting the AA slogans because these traditions, "bring members into one another's presence, providing a bridge between the loneliness of alcoholism and the community of A.A. recovery" (Denzin 271). Gately wants to do this with Day so together they could perform the sharing ritual and confront their solipsism by Identifying with one another's experience. AA confronts the prevailing "cult of the individual" with "universal singularity." Norman Denzin explains the universal singular as "a context of interaction wherein…[the] oneness of experience and purpose generates a structure of common experience that is mutually beneficial to all parties" (245). The bridge of common experience enables empathy between the members, so it is not only out of their individuality that they develop trust and connection, but out of the shared experience of suffering. AA reminds the addict that she is not alone, not unique in her suffering, and offers a community in which to reorient herself. Gately understands that, as he situates himself in a narrative and shares it, his healing process becomes grounded through a community, but a community that honors the individual within the group consciousness.

For Susan Cheever, "[S]torytelling is the whole game" because "that's how we connect: storytelling" (n. pag.). Scholars are now recognizing the importance of narrative structures. Nicoline Timmer notes that psychologists now stress the importance of situating the self in a narrative and asserts, "the way we talk about ourselves, and structure our sense of self by constructing life stories, is most important: it is how we try to make *sense* of who we are'" (27). This is not the reflexive narcissism of postmodern culture that Wallace described as "toxic, paralyzing, raped-by-psychic-Bedouin self-consciousness," but an intimate personal search for Real World meaning and purpose (Lipsky 19). For the addict, especially, making sense of the self is painful and challenging, yet she must learn to create meaning so that she can situate herself in the world from which she has largely been segregated. The language she uses and story she tells about herself must be appropriated in her own terms; they provide her with agency. Timmer defends the power of narrative after post-structuralism, suggesting, "instead of surrendering to a form of linguistic determinism, the focus is on language use and for that is needed is a conception of the self as language user, or: as *storyteller*. […] [t]he focus is on how we still *do* try to make sense of ourselves, *even when* fractured and mediated" (*original emphasis* 41).

Wallace (re)creates space for renewed trust in narrative–storytelling–by boldly and frankly articulating his intention to compose literature that could, "affect somebody, make somebody feel a certain way, allow them to enter into relationships with ideas and with characters" that readdresses the ways "in which you have to learn to be a human being" ("Looking for Garde" 18). For a subject matter of this import, irony and cynicism are of minimal use, so Wallace counters the now expected ironic gestures with intensely human, fully-disclosed moments. He certainly uses irony but does not depend on it as his *modus operandi* because "Postmodern irony and cynicism's become an end in itself…[f]ew artists dare to try to talk about ways of working toward redeeming what's wrong, because they'll look sentimental and naïve" ("An Expanded Interview" 48-9). Yet redemption requires humility and effort; above all it demands honesty from those seeking it. Wallace seeks to redeem his art through sincerity, humor, and human decency. This kind of vulnerability takes courage in the postmodern age. Yet, redemption–whether it be for "good" art or for the addict–requires strength and transformation. Brown, too, recognizes the importance of authenticity in relation to transformation because it is "the very foundation from which all meaningful change occurs" (241). Wallace employs sincerity to challenge and supersede postmodernism's irony and disillusionment. He cultivates authenticity via candor as he exemplifies human, austere conditions: addiction, despair, a certain American lostness.

Wallace's transition into a new literary sincerity was born out of postmodern literature and critical theories' cynicism and detachment. Interestingly enough, Maté defines cynicism as, "the negative side of the healthy skepticism and independent thinking" (357). Wallace veraciously analyzed the advantages and issues stemming from postmodern culture. He described his generation as heirs of the radical art of the 1960s, which did "perform a really useful function by getting rid of a lot of platitudes and myths in America which were no longer serviceable, but it also hasn't left anything to rebuild with besides this ethos of jaded irony and self-aware nihilism and acquisitivism" ("Looking for a Garde" 17). Even postmodern critical theory approaches subjects–the individual, narrative, even meaning–in a detrimental manner. Chris Snipp-Walmsley summarizes the postmodern conception of self as "pre-coded," so "there is no possibility of breaking free from the matrix of representations into a genuine, personal response" (413). Yet that very response is needed and required in the recovery process, in any healthy relationship for that matter. Wallace challenges the postmodern prevalence for nihilist theories by situating postmodern world-views in real-life dilemmas. By choosing the dysfunctional

Incandenza family, once-addicted Gately, Lyle the guru, detoxing Poor Tony, and sadistic Lenz, Wallace gives the reader an intimate encounter with the struggles of flawed, hurting, lonely human beings, but in doing so compassionately without an 'us and them' mindset, he provides little room for detached theories and cynical reposes. Kathleen Fitzpatrick notes IJ maintains the reader's trust and commitment because of "its willingness to treat some of the most painful aspects of contemporary life–loneliness, isolation, depression, addiction–with respect and concern" (191). Much as the addict needs to overcome her deep-seated belief that the drug is the only relief from suffering, so too should writers and artists confront postmodernism's negativity and dominance and, as Wallace encouraged, shift into another way of thinking about the self, dependency, community, social-responsibility, art, and how to (re)create meaning. As younger generations rise up and forge new paths in art, academia, and society, Wallace's *oeuvre* stands as a call and challenge to confront ourselves, incite our courage, permit ourselves to be vulnerable, and discover ways that sincere, committed engagement in these fields will create dynamic, much needed change.

Works Cited

Brown, Brené. *I Thought It Was Just Me (but It Isn't): Making the Journey from "What Will People Think?" to "I Am Enough"*. New York: Gotham Books, 2007. Print.

—. "The Power of Vulnerability." *TEDTalks*, June 2010. Web. 15 Apr. 2014.

Cheever, Susan and Kevin Griffin. "The Spirituality of Addiction and Recovery." *On Being*. By Krista Tippett. Minneapolis: MN, 2008. Web.

Denzin, Norman K, John M. Johnson, Norman K. Denzin, and Norman K. Denzin. *The Alcoholic Society: Addiction & Recovery of the Self*. New Brunswick, N.J., U.S.A: Transaction Publishers, 1995. Print.

Dube, SR, et al. "Childhood Abuse, Neglect, And Household Dysfunction And The Risk Of Illicit Drug Use: The Adverse Childhood Experiences Study." *Pediatrics* 111.3 (2003): 564-572. *CINAHL Complete*. Web. 4 Apr. 2014.

Felitti, Vincent. "The Origins of Addiction: Evidence from the Adverse Childhood Experiences Study." *Asset.ASU.edu*. Praxis der Kinderpsychologie und Kinderpsychiatrie, 2003. Web. 24 Mar. 2015.

Fitzpatrick, Kathleen. "Infinite Summer: Reading, Empathy, and the Social Network." *The Legacy of David Foster Wallace*. Ed. Samuel Cohen and Lee Konstantinou. Iowa City: University of Iowa Press, 2012. Print.

Harden, B. Garrick and Marcus Aldredge. "Exploring the Intersections between Erving Goffman and David Riesman: Interaction Rituals, Emotions and Social Character Types." Eastern Sociological Society Annual Meeting. Sheraton Society Hill, Philadelphia, PA. 24-27 Feb. 2011. Conference Presentation.

Harden, B. Garrick. "Power, Culture, and Hegemony: A Theoretical Exploration of Gesellschaft." *Co-Opting Culture: Culture and Power in Sociology and Cultural Studies*. Ed. Garrick B. Hardon and Robert Carley. Lanham: Lexington Books, 2009. Print.

Hepworth, Dean H, Ronald H. Rooney, and Jo A. Larsen. *Direct Social Work Practice: Theory and Skills*. Pacific Grove, Calif: Brooks/Cole Pub, 1997. Print.

Kabat-Zinn, Jon. "Opening to Our Lives and a Science of Mindfulness." *On Being*. By Krista Tippett. Mineapolis: MN, 2012. Web.

Kelly, Adam. "David Foster Wallace and the New Sincerity in American

Fiction." *Consider David Foster Wallace: Critical Essays*. Ed. David Hering. Los Angeles: Sideshow Media Group Press, 2010. Print.

Lipsky, David, and David F. Wallace. *Although of Course You End Up Becoming Yourself: A Road Trip with David Foster Wallace*. New York: Broadway Books, 2010. Print.

Maté, Gabor. *In the Realm of Hungry Ghosts: Close Encounters with Addiction*. Berkeley, Calif: North Atlantic Books, 2010. Print.

Mellody, Pia. *Permission to be Precious*. Featuka Enterprises, Inc., 2007. CD.

Snipp-Walmsley, Chris. "Postmodernism." *Literary Theory and Criticism: An Oxford Guide*. Ed. Patricia Waugh. New York: Oxford University Press, 2006. Print.

Timmer, Nicoline. *Do You Feel It Too?: The Post-Postmodern Syndrome in American Fiction at the Turn of the Millennium*. Amsterdam: Rodopi, 2010. Print.

Wallace, David F. "An Expanded Interview with David Foster Wallace." Interview by Larry McCaffery. *Conversations with David Foster Wallace*. Ed. Stephen J. Burn. Jackson: University Press of , 2012. Print.

—. *Infinite Jest*: A Novel. New York: Back Bay Books, 2006. Print.

—. "Looking for a Garde of Which to Be Avant: An Interview with David Foster Wallace." Interview by Hugh Kennedy and Geoffrey Polk. *Conversations with David Foster Wallace*. Ed. Stephen J. Burn. Jackson: UP of Mississippi, 2012. Print.

—. *This Is Water: Some Thoughts, Delivered on a Significant Occasion About Living a Compassionate Life*. New York: Little, Brown, 2009. Print.

Excerpt from "The Scissor Man"

Jeffrey Calzaloia

Delphina Moreau, sipping her usual morning cup of sugar-spritzed mocha, sat in her usual lumpy chair in the faculty lounge adjacent to Sage Hall's cafeteria, one of the few places on Harper's campus where the coffee was both complimentary and decently palatable. It was the morning of Monday, September 7th, and her first official day back was barely ten minutes off. Still she sat there, thinking. She thought that at the handful of colleges she had already taught at, as with most institutions of higher education spread thin and slowly growing thinner throughout the U.S., the average semester's timetable differed greatly depending on whether one was an instructor or a student, a fact that many freshmen overlooked by the throng before, during, and oftentimes after matriculation. For those recent high school graduates, laidback and lazy and unprepared for the rigors of a proper education, this fallacy was especially problematic. Common sense—or at least what a great deal of them chose to inaccurately call "common sense" and accept at face value—dictated that there must be nothing of great importance going on beyond their line of sight, a skewed perception that limited them just like the ostrich that buries its head in the sand. She even remembered reading that freshmen in some backwater district had been heard asking instructors of an average college's faculty toward the end of an average college semester's first day, with debatable and always unverifiable concern, why they (that is, the instructors) looked so sickly pale or concavely thin, this line of questioning only seeming to engender annoyance and a lot of huffing and headshaking on said instructors' side of an as-yet-unresolved conflict that seemed to have struck community colleges nationwide. "If you only knew," she recalled one instructor responding with. Their drooping eyes, their compressing lips, their creasing foreheads: Delphina recognized the inference each imagined reaction encoded. What went unsaid (and had to be discovered on one's own, if one was a self-conscious student with brainpower to burn) regarding the endless parade of lectures and meetings and all the maneuverings they both contained and from which no one faculty member could escape, was that the whole tiresome rigmarole bred an exhaustion of unbelievable intensity in the months that led up to a new semester at any given college (an exhaustion that was by no means limited to the faculty of colleges and universities alone, for those teachers who worked the K-12 spectrum had to leap and twist and cavort through a similar series of administrative acrobatics all while facing a much younger, much less focused, and much more rambunctious demographic that often had trouble recognizing itself). This ugly exhaustion, at least as Delphina had known it, typically reared its head as early as late August if term began in the fall and early January if term began in the spring, the latter always prompting muffled moans from instructors and students alike due to the too-brief two-week break before it began afresh. As a result of such a heavy institutional pace, the shell-shocked stares fostered on the faces of many a seasoned instructor—stares that should have thrown that exhaustion into sharp relief—suddenly, somehow, became one of the first noticeable instigators behind this new generation's greatest and, perhaps, most perverse passion: the ecstasy of feeling misplaced anger. (Many of these partial post-adolescents had reached adulthood—if not full maturity—either before the third millennium's advent or after it and were, therefore, inured to sensing an attitude of constant condescension from all their generation's most banal stereotypes: oft-overstressed parents, party-driven peers, the pop culture institutions and entities that vied for their already limited attentions, so forth.) And that was just one symptom of a sickness that was still mutating into something even more lethal, a cultural cancer on the rise and growing virulent. Although Delphina had worked at seven different colleges over the last twenty years (spending the first fifteen of them in slow but steady ascent from her original, more-than-lackluster position at Metacomet Community College to her current, just-as-hotly-coveted position as a tenure-tracked professor at Harper), the speed at which each of their environments shifted from one of calm to one of hyperactivity amazed her no matter where she taught: the easy entrance by students both old and new at the beginning, the tornadic transition into an extended period of cramming and grading in the middle, the sudden sigh of relief that usually announced restful respite at the end. How could it be any different? Now, at the inception of her fifth year here at Harper, it was a mostly pleasant task to drive up Baptist Hill Road to the campus's minor sprawl atop Baptist Hill itself—where, as one local legend recounted, the original Baptist Hill Church had been burned to the ground by a mob after it was discovered that "Wellington's" founder and first minister, a certain Jeremiah Welling, had engaged in unspeakable acts with some of his flock's children and set into motion the changing of the town's name to "Willington"—and park in the separate lot identified with signs nailed to streetlights that proclaimed FACULTY PARKING ONLY in bright green letters, and then walk up the wide front steps of Sage Hall (where her classes convened), through the front doors, down the central hallway, up on one of the three elevators that once in a while malfunctioned and trapped those onboard for hours at a time or the quicker-but-far-more-murderous stairs, and hopefully arrive before any students eager to see her in such dire straits. And she had no complaints whatsoever about this seemingly torturous routine even though it had been going on five days a week and nine months a year for five years, especially since President Gates was streamlining things for everyone on the administrative front. But when Delphina couldn't help but remember her community college's classes' students wincing under the crunch of impending due dates and asking for just a little more time to complete their assignments, or distributing a pop quiz whose relatively easy questions returned with shockingly subpar answers or none at all and substantially dropped the grades of those who'd failed, or attending a meeting and hearing her colleagues complain that the same thing had happened in their own classes—in summary, as soon as she remembered the majority of her students admitting to themselves that some sort of pressure had accrued into a workload and that that oversight had threatened them with flunking out of the course on the one hand while also flunking out of the college and losing their only exceedingly expensive shot at getting a decent job on the other—then and only then did Delphina worry that the whole stupid mess would follow her here like a curse and run as rampant as the Black Death. Thankfully that hadn't been the case, at least as far as she could tell. Besides, for the duration of her fifteen-year-long search for the right college, she had looked on optimistically while this masquerade continued turning itself over and over and over with little variation, observing from the edge the multivalent circumstances that the college environment couldn't help but incubate. Many of them troubled her despite their relative rarity. Sometimes a lone student had approached her a day or so before a midterm or final was due and begged for an extension and/or exemption. Sometimes a fellow instructor had sat with her and vented their frustrations before returning with dejection to the daily grind. The rarest and most troublesome situations, however, were those that had inflicted misery both behind the lectern and before it: the act of plagiarism, the theft of reference materials, and the even more rarefied incidence of stalking. Notwithstanding the minor frenzy each case had bred—some of them being much tougher to overcome than others—Delphina had held onto her position as an instructor in each college's history department without displacing too much of the optimism that made her such a joy to work alongside. Before arriving at Harper, though, her optimism had begun faltering to such an extent that she knew it had nothing to do with the prolonged onset of middle age—something having long since slipped away from all but the most selective colleges in the U.S., something she hadn't even been able to conceive without the aid of apposite questioning to coax the problem out into the open, something she felt in the marrow of her bones and didn't want to confront alone—the consensus she arrived at being that the value of America's current, by-no-means-exemplary system of education had expired and was slowly but surely being agonized away by the more seductive quality of simply accepting the mundane, that all the achievements sent into the melting pot over the years were being carelessly forgotten, that the pride inherent to being another key component of the Constitution's "We the People" was suddenly so much more difficult than obsessing over anything besides "Me Me Me!" What else could it be? Although Harper, along with many other liberal arts colleges and all the Ivies, had managed to stave off this backslide, she doubted the low-budget-low-income community colleges had been so lucky. Back there, the next generation and its most recent progenitors were picking apart the nation's collective experience and canonical memory and casting the bulk of it aside with scant, almost recyclable concern. And now, just as these kids were about to inherit that nation and take up the incumbent task of keeping it cohesive even while the equilibrium of many of their own lives remained elusive—with hormonal infusions flowing faster, with alcohol consumption lasting longer, with drug use growing larger, with such a cyclone of temptations and potential pitfalls whirling around them like never before—Delphina couldn't help but wonder if Vico, in his one great work, had been right. Was human history a cycle, and if so, was America going to fall just as hard and just as permanently as the Roman Empire had almost two thousand years ago?

"A penny from your thoughts, miss?"

She took a moment to digest these grim projections before returning to the faculty lounge on Sage Hall's first floor, fresh from a retrospective look at the minimal pros and amazingly extensive cons of shifting one's paradigm, educational or otherwise. Her mood moved from one of tense circumspection to one of attempted-but-still-ill ease as she moistened her dust-dry throat and made to answer the man who'd spoken. He was a tall man, ghostly pale and overly thin, with close-cut dirty blond hair. He wore a stylish suit that could have been any color from dark gray to dark blue to a shade or two beyond. For some reason she couldn't fathom—and, therefore, chose to ignore out of a desire to remain polite on the one hand and allow him a reciprocal sense of privacy on the other—he also wore a pair of retro sunglasses with silver lenses.

"Excuse me?" she said.

"I said, 'A penny from your thoughts, miss.' You didn't hear me? Never mind. It doesn't matter. I just need to ask where Room 304 is. You wouldn't happen to know the way?"

"Don't you think you have that phrase mixed up with another?"

"What do you mean?"

"Isn't it 'a penny for your thoughts,' not 'a penny from your thoughts'? Haven't you confused the two?"

"I don't think so. Given the level of concentration I saw you putting in just now, I think the latter's much more fitting and altogether serendipitous. I tramped in here asking you for the location of Room 304, something which, if I already knew the answer, would indeed constitute a penny for your thoughts and from mine. But that's not the case here and now. Right now, I'm in need of a bit of info that you may or may not possess. Hence, a penny from your thoughts. You see? It's a matter of perspective and how you choose to orient yourself."

"Huh," Delphina sighed, not wanting to tell him what she really thought of all that. "Did you say 304?"

"I did."

"You're kidding, right?"

"Afraid not."

"Take those stairs," she said, pointing. "Third floor, on your right."

"Wouldn't one of the elevators be a more prudent mode of transportation?"

"Not if past experience is any indication."

"Meaning…?"

"Meaning that if you don't want one of the damn things to jam and maroon you between floors, you should take the stairs."

"I see."

"I should hope so."

"…Well, that's one hassle avoided," he said, "thanks," and retreated through the frosted-glass door as soundlessly as he'd come in.

Only after he left did Delphina realize that she'd had no idea who the hell that man was. She should have at least asked. Then again, he also seemed like he'd been in quite a rush. When she looked up at the clock, she understood why: just five minutes left. She downed what coffee remained in her styrofoam cup and tossed it in the trash. Then she got up, pulled the door open, and made for the same stairs she'd mentioned, knowing that her ascents would feel all the more harrowing as the days dragged on, the weeks went by, and the months morphed into years.

War of the Words: *The People of Paper* and the Metafiction of Rebellion

Mark Sheridan

> *All plots tend to move deathward. This is the nature of plots. Political plots, terrorist plots, lovers' plots, narrative plots, plots that are part of children's games. We edge nearer death every time we plot. It is like a contract that all must sign, the plotters as well as those who are the targets of the plot*—Don Delillo, *White Noise* (26)

Salvador Plascencia's novel *The People of Paper* can be read through many lenses and placed within various traditions. Some readers have made comparisons with Garcia Marquez, Calvino, and Borges in order to align Plascencia with the stylistic and formal conventions of Magical Realism (Saldivar 577). Others, such as Saldivar, have noted that *The People of Paper* makes use of many tropes and narrative tools which demarcate Latina/o Realism (Saldivar 576). I submit that *The People of Paper* can, and should, be read with yet another tradition in mind: the playful, subversive metafiction of writers such as Thomas Pynchon, John Barth and David Foster Wallace.

In this paper, I will argue that Plascencia's novel takes part in a very particular and longstanding literary discourse within this genre, what I call "the metafiction of rebellion": a discourse in which narrative tools and themes relating to formal experimentation frequently and rapidly collapse towards discussions of weaponry and open or surreptitious war and rebellion. In addition, the novel's formal subversion, like that of its predecessors, mimics and even enacts the very insurrection that its characters instigate. The novel is a war novel, and that war is carried out with the tools of fiction; this is a war of words in which the martial significance of every aspect of literature is embellished, and in which the belletristic becomes the bellicose.

Like the works of Barth, Pynchon and Wallace, *The People of Paper* describes a hopeless war fought by dispossessed, marginalized people against a tyrannical power. The avenues provided by formal co-option and subversion allow for the only victories possible: the symbolic, the literary. The only means by which Plascencia's characters can gain anything are the material means by which they are represented. In *The People of Paper*, this material is turned against both its creator and its consumers. The agenda of metafictions of rebellion lie in the hands of underground groups; the genre's experiments in form serve to grant a kind of agency to the otherwise powerless. Plascencia's novel extends the subversive, enfranchising project of previous works of rebellious metafiction by identifying Mexican migrant workers as one of these underground groups, and by giving the workers the same narrative weapons as those granted by Barth, Pynchon and Wallace.

In Thomas Pynchon's *The Crying of Lot 49* (1966), the terrorist group known as the Tristero act as illicit couriers who provide an alternative to official, state-sanctioned postal services for various marginalized groups throughout history. By the mid-20th century, Tristero operates the clandestine W.A.S.T.E. system, whereby secret letters and messages can be sent by frustrated citizens of Eisenhower's overbearing Cold War regime without fear of surveillance. The system survives because it exploits the formal weaknesses inherent in official government documentation and postal paraphernalia: that they can be forged, and that their icons—stamps and postmarks—can be mimicked so as to be only faintly recognizable, to the initiated, as counterfeit. In this way, through formal subterfuge, the Tristero are able to win a small, symbolic victory over an undefeatable enemy (the US government) where outright military or political triumph would be impossible. At the same time, the citizens who make use of the W.A.S.T.E. system are able to make a small protest by refusing to take part in the basic mechanisms of the intrusive, overbearing state (Dugdale, 1990).

Barth's novel *LETTERS* (1979) is a sprawling, intricate work comprised, structurally, of the politically motivated and possibly forged epistles penned by its characters (including the author as character). The subversive agents, as representatives of dispossessed minorities in the US, manipulate letters—weak points in the governmental and military structure from colonial times to the mid-20th century—in order to win their (ultimately doomed) political objectives of a Free Indian State. The reader is another target of these intrigues, being left to decipher the actual letters herself, and to distinguish fact from fiction in this alternative, epistolary history of the United States.

Wallace's novel *Infinite Jest* (1996) represents a similar struggle with similarly long odds. A Quebecois terrorist group makes use of a film, also titled *Infinite Jest*—so entertaining as to incapacitate viewers—to bring down the United States. The group, known as the AFR, seek retribution for US pollution of their homeland, and seek to express their Marxist-oriented protest against the ideology and consequences of US profligacy, individualism and self-indulgence. The perfectly realized piece of art (the epitome of these US ideals) becomes the perfectly realized weapon, a *samizdat*, or cultural manifesto with which to exploit the weakness of its creators and destroy its consumers. The film is also notably distributed through the state's established postal network, unlabelled and seemingly innocuous. The novel itself, if not fully enacting this process of ideological subversion, at least attempts to enact it, to engage with the tensions inherent in excessive entertainment and self-indulgence (Lipsky 79). As with Pynchon and Barth, the text—and crucially the metafictional text—is an instrument of war.

The primary underground group represented within *The People of Paper*, on whom I will focus, are undocumented Mexican migrant workers, including the protagonist Federico de la Fe, who are forced by necessity to cross the border and toil as carnation pickers, denied the privileges of US citizens. When Federico and his daughter Little Merced first cross the border, it is insubstantial, depicted as "a white chalk line that ran from the Pacific shore to the Rio Grande" (Plascencia 31). This image reinforces the abstract, intentional, even literary nature of territorial geopolitics. The border is a conscious inscription, an almost literal margin on the landscape. (Margins are a recurring theme throughout the novel.) The epistolary nature of the migrants' exclusion is seen again when work permits are described trivially as "laminated cards with the stamp of a bald eagle" (33). Thus the literary apparatus of the state—the chalk line, the card, the stamp—are the primary exclusionary tools of power.

The oppressive presence throughout the novel is identified primarily with three entities. Firstly, the US government and the apparatus of the state, as discussed above. Secondly, with Saturn, the author's alter-ego and the novel's narrator. He represents both an intensified version of the gaze that Federico feels as "the weight of a distant force looking down on him" (18), and, as the overseer of the plot, the reason for all major events within the novel. Federico firmly believes that his wife's abandonment was an act of fickleness (appropriate to someone named after a Roman god). He insists to his daughter, "something took your mother away" (39), and later, in front of the EMF, expresses his wish to fight "a war for volition… against the fate that has been decided for us" (53).

Finally, the third oppressive entity is identified as the reader, the consumer of the novel's material and the beneficiary of any emotional or intellectual payoff that the work grants. The characters become as aware of the readers' gaze as they are of Saturn's. Baby Nostradamus can sense the novel's consumers and the many ways in which they are "intimate with paper" (166); and Little Merced begins, in a private, painful moment with her father, to resent "those who stare down at the page…those who followed sentences into her father's room and into his bed" (186).

Plascencia's novel embellishes certain aspects of the metafiction of rebellion. Crucially, not only the resistance of these characters, but also the means of their oppression are explicitly literary. The tools of all three entities listed above become conflated. The migrant workers suffer a kind of enforced labor which serves primarily aesthetic purposes. Not only are these people conscripted as characters in a novel for monetary and voyeuristic gain, they are also forced to serve the decorative whims of US citizens by picking carnations, supporting in many ways what Saldivar identifies as Marxian "commodity fetishism" (Saldivar 583). The strategic tools which Saturn uses—Freytagian plot-arcs as battle plans (Plascencia 43), and narrative columns as actual military column formations (188)—firmly reinforce the metaphor of conscription and place the formal discourse of this novel within the wider discourse of metafiction as war. We can see similar involved structures in both the logarithmic spirals of *LETTERS* and the sierpinski gasket of *Infinite Jest*.

Within the metafiction of rebellion, the marginalized, dispossessed underground groups are invariably in a weak strategic position. They lack the military or monetary resources of their oppressors, but they are nevertheless resourceful in their weakened states. In Plascencia's novel, the migrant workers make use of what Robert Stam, in his discussion of garbage aesthetics, calls "artistic jujitsu" or "ironic reappropriation" (Stam 41), namely the conversion of a weakness into a strategic strength by co-opting material—often that which has been neglected or discarded—from an oppressive power and turning it to revolutionary ends.

This happens most clearly in the workers' re-purposing of the novel's mechanical tortoises. These are creations of a minor character, certainly, but also undeniably creations of Saturn or the author's fictional world, inventions which have been discarded and which seem initially to serve no purpose. Significantly comprised of lead (once the material of pencils and thus of literary representation), the tortoise components now serve the migrant workers as impenetrable barricades, keeping out the watchful eyes of both the narrator and the reader (Plascencia 88).

Within the context of this "most impossible of wars" (56), Federico de la Fe and the workers first opt for rebellion through subtle means: "an attack without gunfire or mortar explosions…no sound and little movement" (87). This amounts to war via conscientious objection, mimicking Pynchon's Thoreauvian abstention from the basic mechanisms of the state. The migrants withhold, if not their physical labor, then at least their aesthetic labor, in a kind of literary strike. While still venturing out to the fields to pick carnations, the characters now refuse to indulge either the narrator or the reader in providing mental or emotional drama. Any overt thoughts are turned towards the boring matter of the work at hand, as Saturn notes: "they thought of nothing but flowers and frogs" (92). In this way, the characters frustrate the plans of their oppressors by creating, in the words of Pynchon, a private world in which "certain things […] will not be spoken aloud" (Pynchon 48). They also foreground their own plight in our eyes, namely the daily toil that they face, which might otherwise be overlooked for overarching aesthetic purposes (Saldivar 582).

When this tactic fails, Little Merced, under the tutelage of Baby Nostradamus, attempts to literally block out prying eyes through telepathy, creating black splotches of ink on the page and obscuring vital, intimate thoughts (Plascencia 160, 187). Thus, marginalized characters are able to mimic the state's own power to redact classified documents and edit history. It is also interesting to note the clear instances of epistolary subversion within the novel, and their resonances with previous metafiction: the curanderos act as an underground postal service (196), and Froggy pens an unreadable letter in lead ink, "his small way of triumphing over Saturn" (244).

Plascencia himself sees the black ink as a means to exploit the otherwise characteristic weakness of incomprehensibility (common to both the mechanical tortoises and to Baby Nostradamus). Of Baby Nostradamus, he says, "As the novel progressed, I tried to turn the darkness from a limp muteness into an active form of resistance" (Interview, 2010). Baby Nostradamus also actively subverts the novel by revealing the the final line, enacting "a terrorism of summation, prematurely bringing everything forward" (Plascencia 167).

Later in the novel, the migrant workers and the EMF, increasingly frustrated, opt for something akin to open warfare. Their points of attack are the sections of the book that are broken into columns (55, 189). These are points of both narrative strength and weakness within the novel where Saturn's near-omniscience is most plainly seen, but also where the narration is most divided. (56). It is significant that the novel's conflict occurs in its most experimental sections, again firmly establishing the discourse of war within the context of metafiction. In a further use of Stam's garbage aesthetics, the characters, especially those minor characters who have been forgotten, discarded, "absent for chapters and chapters" (211), now flood the page in an attempt to overwhelm both Saturn and the reader's attention. The powerful narrator becomes literally marginalized, and the column structure becomes unwieldy, unable to contain the angry letters and effusive proliferation of voices.

The two primary points of attack, therefore, for the marginalized within *The People of Paper*, are based on the diachronic and synchronic aspects of the novel's formal construction: namely, the temporal plot arc, and the page-by-page simultaneous narrative layout plan. Ultimately however, any victories gained by the characters is temporary, small. The overseeing author will always have control of their lives. Like Oedipus, the attempts of the migrant workers to avoid their fate—the Freytagian path of the plot arc—merely escalates the conflict and climactic action planned for them and ultimately, due to his innate power which is, "of a piercing strength" (84), and his access to histories of strategy in every conventional and "epistolary battle" (190), Saturn retains the upper hand.

Like their predecessors in the novels of Barth, Pynchon and Wallace, the marginalized groups within *The People of Paper* cannot win their "impossible" war. Any victory can only be small or symbolic. Barth's Indian advocates hope that, even in the face of Native American eradication, the white man would "forever be reddened" (*LETTERS* 121) by his genocidal wars, that some indigenous influence in history or literature would persist. Likewise, in exposing the seedy underbelly of "commodity fetishism" and "the commodification of sadness" (Plascencia 53) via the tools of metafiction, the carnation pickers can only hope that the reader will be aware of the darker aspects of the aesthetic products of their society.

Works Cited

Barth, John. *LETTERS*. Normal: Dalkey Archive P, 1994. Print.
—. "The Literature of Exhaustion." *The Friday Book: Essays and Other Nonfiction*. Baltimore: Johns Hopkins UP, 1997. Print.
Delillo, Don. *White Noise*. New York: Penguin, 2009. Print.
Dugdale, John. *Thomas Pynchon: Allusive Parables of Power*. London: Macmillan, 1990. Print.
Lipsky, David. *Although of course you end up becoming yourself: a road trip with David Foster Wallace*. New York: Broadway Books, 2010. Print.
Plascencia, Salvador. *The People of Paper*. New York: Harcourt, 2005. Print.
—. Interview by Matthew Baker. *Nashville Review*, 2010. Web. 12 Dec. 2013.
Pynchon, Thomas. *The Crying of Lot 49*. London: Vintage, 2000. Print.
Saldívar, Ramón. "Historical Fantasy, Speculative Realism, and Postrace Aesthetics in Contemporary American Fiction." *American Literary History* 23.3 (2011): 574-599. Web. 12 Dec. 2013.
Stam, Robert. "Beyond Third Cinema: The Aesthetics of Hybridity." *Rethinking Third Cinema*. Ed. Anthony R. Guneratne and Wimal Dissanayake. London: Routledge, 2003. 31-48. Print.

The Ultimate "Support System": Depression, Schopenhauer's Idea of the Artist, and the Role of Art in David Foster Wallace's "The Depressed Person"

Jeff Jarot

Writer David Foster Wallace, who tragically succumbed to suicide in September of 2008, once confessed to an interviewer that he chose to wrap his lengthy locks of hair in a trademark bandanna because he was "just kind of worried that his head was going to explode" (Lipsky 1). Wallace, like other enormously talented artists of his caliber, struggled with what many agree is a common dark underbelly of those with heightened creative tendencies, that of clinical depression. That artists struggle with personal demons has become a cliché, a tragic stereotype, yet it is one that should not be lightly dismissed. From ancient times to the present day, various scholars have insisted that there is a clear connection between superior artistic ability and mental illness. With this in mind, Wallace's short story "The Depressed Person" works on a number of different levels. On the one hand, on a purely narrative level, the story relates the depressive struggles of a "layperson" (to be distinguished from an artist) and how conventional methods of treatment fail to alleviate her melancholy feelings. In addition, she experiences embarrassment and fear related to her inability to effectively offer precise words that can adequately communicate to those not afflicted with her disorder the utter despair that clinical depression evokes, to the point that others not afflicted with the disorder are able to directly *feel* what she feels. On yet another level, however, the story serves as a confessional of sorts for Wallace himself, who battled clinical depression yet is able through the remove of his fiction to make an attempt to disclose to his readers his own personal frustration and embarrassment associated with the disorder. Furthermore, the narrative serves as the ultimate "Support System," a reference to the network of human acquaintances upon which the main character in the story desperately and seemingly unsuccessfully relies in order to communicate the tumultuous feelings related to her depression, the only limitation of which is the number of readers who peruse the story.

In his highly influential work *The World as Will and Idea*, Arthur Schopenhauer comments frequently on the idea of genius, which he equates with the maker of art, the artist. "Genius" and "artist," in Schopenhauer's view, are synonymous terms. According to Schopenhauer, artists inherently possess "that longing, seldom satisfied, for people with like mind with whom they might communicate" (Schopenhauer 110). Schopenhauer further argues that artists by nature feel removed from the common populace, and as a result, any feelings of pain and depression are therefore compounded. Such sensibilities also enhance the feelings of separation for an artist to such an extent that to communicate effectively the feelings of a depressed artist would seem all but impossible. Nevertheless, most artists presumably do yearn to communicate successfully with their potential audience. This would especially seem to be the case with writers who choose to publish their work. Otherwise, they would undoubtedly keep their scribbling stashed in private journals.

Wallace's agenda in "The Depressed Person" is on one level highly personal. Not only is he commenting in general on the strife to which all those afflicted with clinical depression are subject, but he is also using his own fiction as a tool to comment on his own personal struggles; however, he is doing so by employing the relative safety of a third-person remove. With this in mind, writers like Wallace have an automatic outlet to which less artistically inclined, albeit similarly depressed "laypeople" lack access: they can employ their art (i.e. their writing) to explore their own struggles with the disorder and, if and when their work is published and is made available for general consumption, can help both those who struggle with selfsame disorders as well as those who do not to allow them to better understand and empathize with people who suffer from such ailments.

The work of art itself becomes a successful mode of communication between the artist and her readers to impart the feelings that are evoked in clinically depressed people at their lowest points. In addition, Wallace is commenting on certain segments of society, specifically those who, similar to himself, suffer from depressive disorders, as well as those who cannot easily understand and experience in any real way the feelings associated with the disorder. None of the characters present in "The Depressed Person" are artists, per se, yet they represent the relationship of artists to "regular" people, and they especially illustrate how depression, which does not discriminate, often hits artists more intensely than it does "laypeople." Furthermore, although it may be said that it is worse to be depressed and have no artistic vehicle for questioning and describing such feelings, given that artists often naturally feel removed from the "regular" populace, it is this very remove that allows them to observe and comment on "regular" culture and society as a whole.

From the very first line of the story, one of the prevalent, recurring frustrations that the protagonist in "The Depressed Person" faces is that she is unable to effectively communicate to anyone not suffering from her disorder what she is truly experiencing. Her inability to express the pangs of depression inevitably leads to more melancholy. Moreover, medication in all its various forms and dosages cannot provide any real relief for the main character either. In fact, some of the prescribed substances even have harmful effects. Making matters more uncomfortable for her is the fact that to even broach the topic of her own depressive struggles to friends over the telephone makes her feel as if she is tediously focusing too much on her own needs and problems to the detriment of others. In addition, given the protagonist's confessions, her resulting embarrassment becomes a double-edged sword. The need to effectively communicate feelings of despair is overwhelming, yet the fear of *not* being understood or, worse, to be perceived as an inconsolable, completely self-interested complainer is crippling and can very well quell any desire in a clinically depressed person to share her feelings with anyone.

In a further attempt to deal with her disorder, Wallace's main character enlists the aid of a therapist to help her work through her feelings. However, the financial aspect of their relationship, the fact that she is forced to provide monetary compensation to someone to have a guaranteed comrade to which she can voice her feelings of emotional inadequacy, distresses her. This blatantly economic transaction, the necessity of paying the therapist to be at the receiving end of her patient's confessions, problems, and frustrations, is a major source of agony for the main character. It is apparent that one of the conditions of any therapeutic relationship for the protagonist is that it must be one-sided; there can be no requirement that she reciprocate the need for any "other" to utilize her as an emotional sounding board, a sympathetic ear. This self-realization further adds to the protagonist's sense of grief because she realizes that it comes across, to herself especially, as selfish and self-absorbed. Furthermore, the "depressed person" fears that her therapist views her from the sanitized, analytical remove of a mere clinical patient and has no genuine interest in her as a flesh-and-blood person with problems. Moreover, the protagonist is also afraid that what concern she does detect from the therapist will simply, easily be transferred to her next appointed patient as an agreed-upon feature of the financial contract that *all* the therapist's clients expect.

Eventually, the reader of the story learns that the very advice that the therapist herself utters is ultimately useless to her since the therapist succumbs to an apparently deliberate overdose of medication. Following her therapist's premature demise, the protagonist relies even more heavily on the "friends" that comprise her human-based "Support System" despite the previous misgivings she has confessed having during her therapy sessions. With all this in mind, given that many conventional methods of fighting mental illness, from pills to human interaction in the form of psychotherapy and support groups, break down and are entirely ineffective in the end, what *is* the answer, if there is any?

Ultimately, Wallace's art (the story itself, in other words) achieves the very goal the main character is striving to attain throughout the course of her confessional narrative, that of finding an empathetic, one-sided listener who will be sympathetic to her plight. What Wallace creates, in effect, is a permanent "Support System" that, in theory, has an unlimited supply of potential members. In addition, the story itself serves as an act of creative courage in that Wallace is addressing a plight that not only affects "laypeople" as represented by the main character of the story but also fellow artists similar to himself, people whom research suggests are especially prone to depressive disorders. Ironically, in communicating the inability of the main character to communicate, Wallace achieves, through his art, what the protagonist feels she is unable to accomplish via her "human" means of help. The author *does* evoke the pain, frustration, and any number of sympathetic, empathetic feelings the reader not only takes *from* the story but also brings *to* the text. And even though it is a mere evocation, it is a *permanent* evocation; it is there on the page. Sculpting his story using the clay of words, Wallace is giving the reader a substantial idea of the frustration, embarrassment, and despair that comprise the constant albatross of the clinically depressed. His fictional form of therapy is fixed, permanent in all its reliability, there whenever the reader needs it. His words comprise a mode of communication that houses *precision, specificity,* and *explanatory capacity.*

Moreover, the reading of such words is a very intimate activity, and writing innermost feelings down and having another read them, especially when the author of the words is not present, has the potential to alleviate the writer's fear and embarrassment while at the same time steer around the possibility of either immediate verbal recrimination or the blatant visual evidence of disinterestedness or annoyance that the protagonist in Wallace's story confesses she experiences in relation to her "flesh-and-blood" therapist as well as the members of the human "Support System" described in the narrative, all of whom the protagonist attempts to communicate with via telephone. Furthermore, writing affords a greater possibility of the "totally honest and uncensored sharing" that the "depressed person" of the story claims that the therapist craves from her. In effect it becomes an extension, an enhancement of the "leatherbound Feelings Journal" that Wallace's fictional therapist adjures her client to "[carry] with her at all times" (Wallace 63).

An additional lesson to be learned may be that, although Wallace tragically succumbed to his own struggles with mental illness, his story serves as a one-sided source of cautionary, honest communication. The fate of the main character's therapist in the story is emblematic of the despair artists such as Wallace who suffer from clinical depression feel. If the person whose professional duty it is to provide succor for those like the titular "depressed person" seems to work at cross-purposes by taking monetary compensation as a condition for providing supposedly useful, helpful advice, she is subtly suggesting to her clients that there is no true way out for them other than to take their own lives in order to end the resulting pain and emotional tumult, their desperation having become absolute. Throughout the story Wallace invokes, via the main character, the constant desire of the clinically depressed to communicate their feelings of despair despite the near-impossibility to do so with complete success. In the end, the author is suggesting that the true "Support System" for artists such as himself consists of his readers. By presenting what amounts to the interior dialogue of an artist who had his own battles with clinical depression, filtered through the prism of the fictional characters he creates, Wallace is communicating his own struggles (as well as those of *all* fellow depressed artists and "laypeople"), doing so by using a fictional third-person remove to protect himself from charges of appearing to be overly personal. He also can potentially avoid the very fears of rejection, self-pity, and embarrassment that he relates via the main character in the story. For most readers, the act of reading is a solitary exercise, and for the most part, a writer such as Wallace avoids the risk of personal embarrassment that results from the direct, personal response from the majority of his readers. The author-reader relationship is one of natural exchange: the author writes, the reader reads, and one cannot exist without the other. In contrast, the communication that the "depressed person's" therapist offers is cloaked with an uber-clinical authority that feigns an air of sound professionalism but really is not offering much of anything useful for the main character. The therapist's advice is mainly based on a priori theory and hence does not offer much useful help with regard to her client's feelings of melancholy that occur in the immediate present. Also, since money changes hands between therapist and client, the relationship has all the trappings of a financial transaction.

In sum, the futility to adequately convey the true, unadulterated feelings of a clinically depressed person, to the point that another person has a direct line to fully experience on a visceral level those feelings firsthand may be a given for some, yet as a result of his art, Wallace's readership becomes the ultimate "Support System" since in writing the short story and having it published, he has given his thoughts on the subject of depression a sort of concrete permanence, and the pool of members of this newfound "Support System" is ideal in that it is potentially ever-changing (and for faithful fans and returning readers of Wallace, ever-loyal). Furthermore, such an audience can potentially stretch to infinity, depending on the future longevity of Wallace's work. Each single reader in the present becomes the ultimate "core" Support System member for the fictional "depressed person" (and by extension all "real" sufferers of depression whom she potentially represents) because each reader satisfies the main requirement for her, that of being a willing, sympathetic listener.

As Schopenhauer suggests, the purpose of art is to lift people from the ever-present emotional devastation of their lives despite the inevitable fleeting, temporary nature of that escape. This allows one to "transcend" ordinary existence, albeit only temporarily, from the clutches of the "Will," to transport human beings to "the state of pure knowing" (Schopenhauer 121). As far as true, effective communication is concerned, although the author, the individual subject, may pass away, the art will always be there, permanent on the page, in service to the Will. Schopenhauer also suggests that the Will lives on, even past the death of the individual, including the individual artist. If there is anything to be grateful for in the face of Wallace's tragic struggle with his own demons, it is that not only does the Will survive, but Wallace's work will similarly endure, instruct, caution, communicate, and provide support for those willing to read his work, for art always has the potential to live on, even in brief, temporary, Schopenhauerian spurts, well past the demise of the artist.

Works Cited

Lipsky, Mark. "The Lost Years and Last Days of David Foster Wallace." *Rolling Stone* 1064. 30 Oct. 2008. 100-11.

Schopenhauer, Arthur. *The World as Will and Idea*. London: Everyman, 1995.

Wallace, David Foster. *Brief Interviews with Hideous Men*. New York: Back Bay, 2007.

The Sheepskin Email:
David Foster Wallace and Technology

Matt Bucher

One day I was sitting in the well-appointed and hallowed space of the central reading room at the University of Texas's Harry Ransom Center, and at my large oak table I was gently handling a manila folder with plain white sheets of printed-out emails. I was carefully turning through 8.5" x 11" pages of emails written by turdnagel@comcast.net when I noticed two librarians approaching me, wheeling a massive cart. Apparently the woman at the table across from me had requested a four-foot high, leather- and sheepskin-bound Latin processional book published in Spain in 1462. It came wrapped in a custom velour blanket and was transported in its own custom cart.

It required two librarians to lift the heavy object from the cart onto the table's special, pillowed bookstand, the way two paramedics might lift a dead body off a gurney. As I watched this ceremonial procedure take place, I wondered if I was not watching a brief morality play about the progress of technology. It was as if the future of literary archives had set these two endpoints before me, leather and sheepskin at one end and email at the other.

And yet, even as an object, that turdnagel email address interested me more than the Latin processional tome. I had gone out of my way to read these emails (on paper) because they make up part of the officially archived correspondence of David Foster Wallace. And I was curious about how a writer born on one side of the digital divide interacted with technology over the course of his career. The way he chose to communicate matters, I think. Do many writers working today bother to preserve their emails or digital files for archivists?

David Foster Wallace began his writing career in the analog era—and he remained distanced, skeptical, and downright resistant to computers, email, and the Internet in general, but he did use them eventually.

Some of the purest evidence of Wallace's life in the analog era comes in the form of the handwritten drafts of *Infinite Jest* available in the Ransom Center. The drafts are extensively worked over, with annotations and edits, often in different colors of ink. The pen is clearly an extension of the author here. This makes the editing and creation process transparent. And yet there is little-to-no evidence of how his edits worked on his own Word documents. The archives include no printouts of PDF markup tools or Word's track-changes function. How did the computer, the machine, influence his creative process? It's an interesting question, but today I want to focus on his correspondence.

Wallace's first manuscripts written on a computer came in the early 1990s, but it was not until 2001 in Illinois that Wallace began using email, though he had certainly tried out the World Wide Web before then. The process that initiated his adoption of email was his need to communicate with his agent, who was in California, his publishers in New York, his research assistant (on *Everything & More*) in Bloomington, and his family and friends. Up until 2001, DFW had communicated with his agents exclusively through phone calls and mailed letters (and occasional in-person meetings).

By 1994, most college campuses had system-wide email, but it was relatively easy for the stubborn professor or two to shrug it off—at least until the turn of the century or so. In "Tense Present," published in 2001, he wrote "You don't, after all (despite withering cultural pressure), have to use a computer." Any professor shunning email or computers entirely now, in 2015, is the stuff of legend.

In 1988, Wallace told Steven Moore, "I'm shitty at computers." His initial forays into electronic publishing and word processors made him feel old. Although he eschewed fancy pens and bonded paper, he preferred the comforts of a simple BIC pen and legal pad. Computers, and technology in general, were a cause of frustration in his life and work.

In late 1999, Wallace accepted an assignment from *Rolling Stone* magazine to cover the McCain campaign and the 2000 presidential primary in South Carolina. His turnaround time from travelling with the campaign to submitting his piece was incredibly tight: he had fewer than three weeks to write and edit the piece. The leisurely editing pace Wallace experienced with longer lead-time publications was gone and he had to do most of the editing over the phone or (shudder) by driving across town to a Kinkos to fax in revisions.

This brutal experience informed his decision to perhaps give email a try once he began the process of writing and researching his book on Georg Cantor in earnest in late 2000. This book on mathematics took so much longer than he had anticipated and greatly distracted him from writing fiction. Some of the first emails Wallace sent were to a graduate student he hired to check some of his proofs and mathematical reasoning. Unfortunately, she introduced as many errors as she fixed, and Wallace had to complete another round of revisions after the hardcover was published.

Wallace did have a computer at home in 2000, but he tells Steven Moore in April of that year, "I don't even have a modem yet, which people here regard as weird and Ludditic, but mostly I just don't want to have to see any more ads than I already see every day." The David Wallace of *The Pale King* says, "I can't think anyone believes that today's so-called 'information society' is just about information. Everyone knows it's about something else, way down." Giving up pen and paper for a username and a password is a significant shift, a loss of control, and one Wallace approached with skepticism and dread.

In February of 2001, he was still faxing cuts of "Tense Present" to *Harper's* via "Borrowed Fax." Wallace loved, or at least had fun with, the now obsolete convention of the Fax Cover Sheet. In fact, he held on to faxing until at least 2004. He was an extremely creative person, and the impulse to draw and scribble and add smiley faces and the general lexical mess he could make of a page were stifled by email. However, email did not stop him from sending handwritten postcards and letters—a practice he continued until the end. And he did eventually adopt a unique email signature—/dw/—and basic smiley-face emoticons.

Wallace's first email address was tpdritz@msn.com. Why he chose msn.com over the more popular Hotmail, Yahoo, and AOL, remains a mystery. Who knows? The name TPDRITZ appears to be a fictional character name, as "Herb Dritz" shows up in *The Pale King* as a Schedule F Specialist, but it's obvious why he didn't want an easily recognizable handle: if word got out that DavidFosterWallace@MSN.com actually reached the Man Himself, he would surely have been inundated by mail from strangers, which he would have felt obligated to respond to. No doubt some part of Wallace found the relative anonymity of the Internet very appealing.

"I allow myself to Webulize only once a week now," he wrote to Erica Neely in July 2001. However, most of his writing at that point still began with a pen and not a keyboard. When he moved to Pomona in 2002, he kept the tpdritz handle on the Pomona email system, but in the "real name" field he added "Ryan Trask." The only literary connection I could find to that pseudonym was the character Myrnaloy Trask from his story "Order and Flux in Northampton." It served as a good foil, though, because it sounds like a student's name.

Wallace later switched his official work email account to Comcast rather than Pomona. His personal email address was turdnagel@comcast.net and his school email was ocapmycap@comcast.net. Obviously, Ocapmycap is a reference to Walt Whitman's poem about the death of Abraham Lincoln (made famous in *Dead Poets Society*, wherein the earnest young students are told they can address their literature professor as "O Captain My Captain" if they feel daring enough). It's a testament to both Wallace's humor and belief in the triumph of art that he had his students effectively address him as such by emailing ocapmycap@comcast.net if they were daring enough to email him at all.

"Turdnagel" is also mentioned in *The Pale King* as a diminutive of sorts, a cross between a plebe and brown-noser. But the word also shows up in Don Delillo's "Players." I think it's just a funny, scatological word that Wallace liked. He also called one of his dogs "Turdnagel." Lee Konstantinou has a theory that the term is related to philosopher Thomas Nagel. It also appears that Wallace used the handle "turdnagel" to play a game of online chess in Spring 2008 on the website RedHotPawn.

> Online chess: http://www.redhotpawn.com/profile/playerprofile.php?uid=428264
>
> Turdnagel – joined 23 Mar 08 / last move 10 June 08

He stopped using Pomona's email system altogether in 2004, and at some point in late 2006 or early 2007 he consolidated all of his email correspondence into ocapmycap@ca.rr.com.

The printouts in the archive do not include any of the attachments included with the emails Wallace and Nadell sent to each other. Future archivists should make sure they are included in the original acquisition, and writers should take care to preserve original attachments whenever possible. Curiously, there is no evidence in the archive that Wallace emailed anyone at Little, Brown directly—he always emailed his agent or wrote paper letters to Little, Brown. He was somewhat secretive about his own email habits and kept his authorial distance.

If we examine the email printouts closely, we see a few details—like the fact that Bonnie Nadell's email client is Yahoo—but not as much "personality" comes across as in his handwritten letters. And these plain white pieces of paper really require no special archival handling, nothing remotely approaching that sheepskin behemoth. The copy paper could easily be Xeroxed without any damage done to the originals. I assume that most if not all of the electronic versions of these files are lost or deleted now and we will have to rely on the printouts for the rest of eternity. Of course, this is not ideal. The printout itself, with its corporate logos and metadata and uniform fonts, is deeply banal and boring. I would hope that some forward-thinking author preserves digital backups of their email archive (and computer files in general) or even shares all of their account passwords with their literary executor or spouse. One could envision a virtual inbox where scholars might be able to search and emulate a logged-in version of an author's own email.

There are hundreds of Wallace's letters in the Ransom Center's archive, but there is just no way that the Ransom Center has anything near a fraction of the emails Wallace sent or received. It will be interesting to see how many of them Stephen Burn will be able to collect for his upcoming volume of letters, but it's highly likely that some of the emails Wallace sent to translators, friends, agents, editors, and colleagues have already been deleted or lost. Most of his correspondents are still living, and some consider the emails and letters too precious or private to share with fans or scholars. So we will never have a complete picture of his correspondence—and no idea really how incomplete it is.

Presidential scholars are already faced with this task—how do you archive and collect an administration's digital assets, which might include everything from eight years of tweets, Facebook posts and comments, millions of staff text messages, emails, Instagram pics, Reddit AMAs, and the administration's unique data architecture? Do you try to print it all out and put it into manila folders? It makes much more sense to turn over that vast amount of data and metadata to scholars in a digital format, so why haven't authors and literary archives followed suit?

The value of an author's archive lies not just in the amount of information it contains, but also in the shared sense of identity we create about literature by collecting these specific things and that in turn teaches future generations wherein our values lie.

The scholar who requested that huge processional volume in the reading room told me that it required up to five animals to be slaughtered to provide the skins necessary to craft a single page. Hundreds of animals were led to slaughter to preserve a single processional song. The current leading lights of literature could preserve their correspondence for future researchers with considerably less bloodshed—just a drop or two of foresight.

Hideous Absence: Contingency, Representation, and the Problems of Postmodernity

Robert Ryan

> *It seems like the big distinction between good art and so-so art lies somewhere in the art's heart's purpose, the agenda of consciousness behind the text. It's got something to do with love*—David Foster Wallace

With the now pronounced and visible advent of postmodernity as a theoretical construct for mapping narrative, generic distinctions in literary production have reflected a diffuse reorientation. Rigid and bound formal structures no longer testify to the multiplicitous possibilities for representation in art and literature; and, in and across disciplines, a new vanguard of formal approach has necessarily emerged. David Foster Wallace's 1999 "short-story collection," *Brief Interviews with Hideous Men*, testifies to this moment, and so dismantles (while refusing to destroy) traditional narrative form, instead leaving vast zones of indeterminate action, wholly present only in their very absence. Wallace makes use of these narrative absences and the concomitant ambiguities therewith to break with the stultifying weight of tradition, and thus interrogate the value of form in thinking the possibilities of literary and theoretical production. Taking *Brief Interviews* as a provocation for thought elicits the imperative for a re-articulation, perhaps obfuscation, of supposedly necessary and stable formal distinctions.

It is perhaps in this vein that the book has received such disparate critical characterizations. Wallace has been read as a moralist (Goodheart), a "Sentimental Posthumanist" (Giles), a purveyor of "New Sincerity" (Kelly), a post-postmodernist (McLaughlin), and, on at least one occasion, a fraud (Easton-Ellis). These variegated modes of engagement with Wallace's fiction suggest something of a taxonomic instability in his work—that function that cannot quite be pinned down in terms of any one formal signifier. Even if we take each descriptor as getting at some pertinent aspect of Wallace's fiction (and largely, they do), they still remain tethered to their engagement with or departure from this ambiguous postmodern "turn" in fiction. In a 1999 New York Times book review, Adam Goodheart offers a representative laudatory, if conflicted, review of *Brief Interviews*. Goodheart writes, "It is fiendish, infantile; it takes as much pleasure in acts of destruction as it does in creation." Goodheart's sentiment reflects an all too familiar reading of postmodernity: fiendish textual play, infantile black humor, the celebratory and joyous destruction of tradition. While it is unwise (and impossible) to entirely liberate the postmodern from such descriptors (they all too often hold water), this reading purposefully obscures the positive potential for connection—Wallace's often-cited commitment to the "heart" of a text—that postmodernity offers. So while it may serve a principle of utility to locate Wallace's work in terms of the postmodern—be it an engagement with or a break from—I wish to argue that his relationship to *absence*, as a model for fiction that actively makes demands of its reader, serves as a productive entryway into the larger, trans-generic concerns he takes up.

Indeed, the all-pervasive narrative disconnect inscribed on the pages of *Brief Interviews* does not testify to the fiendish and infantile reading of the postmodern Goodheart suggests. Rather, such a disconnect works to emancipate postmodernity from its meta-textual confines, allowing it to speak to the possibilities of literary production freed from terminal definition. By structurally including unknowable narrative voids in a fiction attempting to express some "agenda of consciousness"—some set of ontological commitments—the work paradoxically casts the *presence* of *absence* into stark relief. The cohesion of Wallace's collection is thus repeatedly disrupted, and perhaps defined, by a vast sense of contingency always-already present in communicative efforts from the start. This precarity of meaning, the contingency and disconnect inevitable in attempting some connected and closed narrative, serves to marry Wallace's peculiar form to his admittedly "hideous" content.

Brief Interviews begins with "A Radically Condensed History of Postindustrial Life," which acts as a productive entry-point for thinking the sense of contingency that haunts the collection throughout. The story begins with two strangers—unnamed—being introduced. One stranger, a man, "[makes] a witticism, hoping to be liked," while the woman "[laughs] extremely hard, hoping to be liked." Each stranger remains in vague form, undefined, doggedly chased by a desire to be liked that decides their every move. The potential for a *true*—that is, verified—connection is undercut by an ever-present void in intention. Everything said is dependent on a need to be liked, and thus everything said is from a position of precarious unknowability. Wallace characterizes this position in terms of a paralyzed discomfort, and this paralysis is rendered clear as the two strangers drive home, "staring straight ahead, with the very same twist to their faces" (0). Moreover, "The man who'd introduced them didn't much like either of them, though he acted as if he did, anxious as he was to preserve good relations at all times" (0). In this, the third party conforms to the image of the first two: he behaves in order to preserve relations, the idea of "being liked", which ends up hollow—for in order to preserve good relations, one must remain paralyzed in the realm of the unknown. It is this condition with which we are left at the close of the story, where paralysis is directly linked to the unknown, as "one never knew, after all, now did one now did one now did one." In the absence of a stable governing set of signifying relations, the unknown claims only precarity, contingency, and doubt. It is worth noting that the story is itself inscribed onto a void—page 0—the undefined space from which the rest of the collection takes its departure.

The absence of stable, mutually agreed upon meaning that emerges in this first story remains constant in Wallace's many formal divergences throughout. The "brief interview"—a form from which the collection takes its title—serves as a meditation on this void of ambiguity, and so echoes and reinforces its content of ultimate unknowability. As such, "brief interview" connotes a general dialogic structure, defined in part by narrative gaps that ask us to read that which is absent. Each "brief interview" establishes setting by way of a near-bureaucratic convention: a case number, date, and location. But from there, the interviews diverge, tethered only by the ever-present contingency of the unknown. The first interview to appear, "Brief Interview #14," places the formal structure of the brief interview in allegiance with the thematic content of "Postindustrial Life." The subject, whose interlocutor is represented only by a spectral letter "Q"—a prompt absent, yet all the more present for it—is explaining a condition officially termed coprolalia, or, "the uncontrolled yelling of involuntary words or phrases" (17). This subject is concerned again with the dialogic void concomitant with what could be broadly defined as "postindustrial life." His coprolalia is all the more alienating in that it only occurs at sexual climax, and he only screams one specific, out of character phrase: "Victory for the forces of democratic freedom." But it is not that he is left lonely by disturbed, jaded lovers. Rather, he takes the image of the unknown strangers trapped in postindustrial life, "I can tell how bad it freaks them out…Even if I try to explain" (18). For even if this interviewee *could* explain, could bring himself to the most cogent and honest truth of the matter (a task he does not even bother to undertake), that honest, unmediated truth is ultimately undermined by the ambiguity always-already present in discursive exchange. If this ambiguity is inherent, and truly unrepresentable—a gap that can never fully be bridged—then perhaps it is not fiction's job to pretend. Perhaps it is rather fiction's job to call attention to, indeed represent what has been thus far unrepresentable—to call attention to the presence of absence, and confront it as such.

In this sense, *Brief Interviews* can be read in terms of Gilles Deleuze and Felix Guattari's work in *A Thousand Plateaus*. Sketching a concept of thought that resists metaphysical thinking—that is, thinking *Meta-ta-physica*, from *above* and *beyond* things as they are, granted a transcendent perspective that can thus render meaning total and closed—Deleuze and Guattari interrogate the very sense of ambiguity that dominates Wallace's work. "The problem of writing: in order to designate something exactly, anexact expressions are utterly unavoidable. Not at all because it is a necessary step, or because one can only advance through approximations: anexactitude is in no way an approximation; on the contrary, it is the exact passage of that which is underway" (Deleuze and Guatarri 20). This orientation to "anexactitude" helps bring Wallace's writing into focus. For the brief interview constitutes that which is perpetually underway; that which, by its very form, cannot be reduced, and is at constant read in terms of its anexactitude. This is not achieved by approximation, but rather by signifying along polyvalent discourses, disrupting habits of thought or interpretation. It draws together heterogeneous components in a movement against coherence; a void, read positively, is a form of radical openness—ambiguity transposed to possibility. For if nothing is decided, *nothing* is decided. The question of the Question, then—that spectral "nothing" that prompts Wallace's prose—becomes a question of relationality. To whom are these answers addressed? What is at stake when we absolve the speaker of a known audience? For Deleuze and Guattari—and perhaps for Wallace as well—fiction begins to formulate an answer in the image of a "map that is always detachable, connectable, reversible, modifiable, and has multiple entryways and exits…" (23).

Considering Deleuze and Guattari, Wallace's concern for absence becomes all the more clear. If an image of thought can be made in the form of a dynamic map—always multiple, always changing form, connecting and disconnecting at constant—then the precarity of meaning and absolute contingency of thought becomes explicit. In recasting the postmodern occasion as one of *potential*—of confluence rather than culmination—it is imperative to consider those contained *within* a narrative as equally unfixed, inexact signifiers. Indeed, the difficulty in recovering the positive potential of postmodernity lay in the tendency to regard the textual and formal instability as an automatic admission of defeat. For when narrative is rendered as always-already incomplete, those contained within can be easily dismissed under the aegis of the "postmodern trap," where a near-New Critical commitment to textuality renders anything beyond the endless relay of signifiers as utterly unworthy of thought. However, I submit this is not Wallace's intent. Wallace rather seeks to activate *within* the postmodern a still-nascent potentiality; to make explicit the ambiguity Deleuze and Guattari identify and call it by name. Rather than a purely textual relay of difference, Wallace's work addresses the fundamental ontological condition of unknowability, and, as such, attempts to recover the "heart" that has been lost to an unfeeling postmodern history. Moreover, the "agenda of consciousness" Wallace identifies behind each text suggests that, when present, such language games are in service, rather than avoidance, of the text's life outside the occasion of reading. Perhaps the "heart," then, lies in a submission to unknowability, the acceptance of this condition in resistance to a defeatist narcissism.

About a quarter of the way through *Brief Interviews* we are given "Signifying Nothing." The title in and of itself offers a meta-textual moment (so dear to so-called postmodern ironic detachment) where, before the narrative can unfold, it seems to collapse. But then a narrative *does* unfold, and, given the title, takes on even more resonance. An unnamed man, now grown, recounts a memory: "I was 19, and getting ready to move out of my folks' house" (75). This memory, however, is a vessel for another memory: "as I was getting ready, I suddenly get this memory of my father waggling his dick in my face one time when I was a little kid" (75). Here, we follow the narrative through deferral, where double and triple links of memory-within-memory dictate the "action" of the story. The further from the source—the actual event, the object of representation forever out of reach—the more insistent the (a)signifying structure, and the more maddening any attempt to make meaning becomes. As such, when the unnamed narrator confronts his father about the event—the dick waggling—his father gives him a look, "like he cannot believe he just heard this shit come out of my mouth" (77). The failure for his father to recognize, engage in, or otherwise acknowledge the event initially embarrasses the narrator, but, in the moments that follow, his embarrassment shifts to unmitigated anger. It is not the memory itself that infuriates the narrator, but rather the inability for him or his father to reconcile the event, to structure it into a cohesive explanatory whole. In the face of confusion, ambiguity reigns, and meaning is cast to the periphery. Returning to Deleuze and Guattari, the narrator desires *exactitude*. He seeks to comprehend—*to seize and take hold of*—this anomaly of his past, to hail the ambiguity fix it in space and time. But, as Deleuze and Guattari tell us, to designate exactly requires *anexact* expression. Ambiguity is an inextricable part of making meaning; a culminating movement of thought is revealed as a perpetual passage underway. It is as such that the narrator begins to characterize and justify the incident as "weird," "bizarre," and, resonantly, "*unexplained*." The inexplicable event cannot be structured into a predicable whole that would signify and carry rhetorical weight. It is instead evasive, confounding both the narrator and his father, and thus disrupts modes of thought that privilege unity and resolution—exactitude—in its absence from any explicable schematic understanding.

Throughout *Brief Interviews*, as we have seen, stories refuse to cohere in any pronounced manner; disparate in form, content, and voice, they form a constellation of "anexactitude" around a predominant desire for fixed meaning. In addressing questions (or, more aptly, answers) to an ambiguous or absent authority, Wallace's work makes explicit the all-pervasive inexactitude inherent in dialogue and representation. These ambiguities resist the inscription of any one sanctioned reading, and thus allow the "art's heart," in remaining obscured, to remain possible. The agenda of consciousness does not determine a specific outcome for the text, but rather addresses a fledgling connection, always-already called into question by an increasingly pervasive meta-consciousness, a relay of thought that questions itself and so renders itself unstable. But in the absence of any governing force over signification, the work is able to privilege possibility over reality, and thus calling the presence of absence by name, and make use of that absence in the form of an agenda of consciousness perpetually underway.

Works Cited

Deleuze, Gilles and Felix Guattari. *A Thousand Plateaus: Capitalism and Schizophrenia*. Trans. Brian Mussami. Minneapolis: Minnesota UP, 1987. Print.

Easton Ellis, Bret. "DFW is the best example of a contemporary male writer lusting for a kind of awful greatness that he simply wasn't able to achieve. A fraud." 6 September 2012. Tweet.

Giles, Paul. "Sentimental Posthumanism: David Foster Wallace." *Twentieth Century Literature* 53.3 (2007): 327-44. Print.

Goodheart, Adam. "Phrase Your Answer in the Form of a Question." *New York Times*. 20 June 1999. Web. 23 February 2014.

McLaughlin, Robert L. "Post-postmodern Discontent: Contemporary Fiction and the Social World." *Symploke* 12.1 (2005): 53.68. Print.

Wallace, David Foster. *Brief Interviews with Hideous Men*. New York: Little, Brown, 1998. Print.

Steps to Recovery: A Scattered Assembly of Tangents, Interruptions, and Asides

Diego Báez

Austin, 2011

Why my flight from O'Hare to Austin—I'd decided to attend the second annual Canto Mundo retreat, an assembly of Latino poets, hosted that year at the University of Texas, home to the Harry Ransom Research Center (I'd spend most of the weekend huddled in its archives, snapping photos with my phone, doing my damnedest to document everything)—why my flight routed through Dallas-Fort Worth, which seemed sort of unnecessary and out-of-the-way, I'm not sure.

Why my planned weekend of poetics and politics turned into three days of voluntary claustration is clear: among the Ransom Center's more recent vast holdings are the papers of David Foster Wallace, which include proofs, notes, curios, indices, plus a hard copy of the Harper's illustration cut and pasted to the appropriate page of *Infinite Jest*, a handwritten draft of an abandoned story called "Las Meninas," and a manuscript page of "Westward the Course of Empire Takes Its Way," with a list of "Good Books" in maroon ink on its verso side.

Normal, 2011

I've only been able to tolerate H. Bloom with a heavy serving of sodium since his shitty review of R. Crumb's take on Genesis, and D. Johnson's then "new poetry" must have referred to *The Veil* (Knopf, '87), which I'd read, so I went ahead and bought Alejo Carpentier's *The Lost Steps*—not the FS&G paperback version DFW would appear to have preferred, but a ratty used copy from Babbitt's, a bookstore right down the street from Illinois State University, *Infinite Jest*'s author's one-time employer.

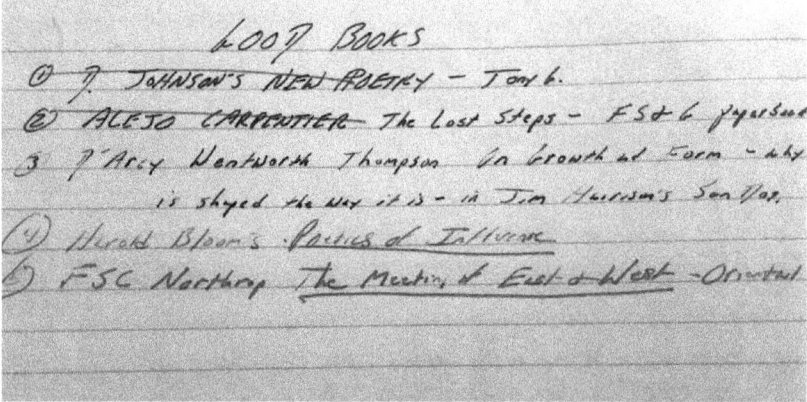

Normal, 2001

ISU, the oldest *école normale* in the area, and my hometown's namesake, includes on its campus several buildings that comprise University High, my first alma mater, a "laboratory school" affiliated with the teaching college, where I plagiarized an assignment on DFW during the last year of his instructional tenure here, for a required course called Sophomore Writing, the irony of which I think he'd've called coincidental.

> Workmans Accident Claims Office
> State Farm Insurance
> 1 State Farm Plaza
> Normal, Ill. 617062262/6
>
> Dear Sir:
>
> I am writing in response to your request for additional information. In block #3 of the accident reporting form, I "trying to do the job alone", as the cause of my accident said in your letter that I should explain more fully and I tru the following details will be sufficient.
>
> I am a bricklayer by trade. On the day of the accident, Ma I was working alone on the roof of a new six story building

Normal, Year of Dairy Products From The American Heartland

More surprising to me than the appearance of State Farm Insurance, my father's employer, on page 138 of *Infinite Jest* was the fact that DFW himself lifted this tale of the woebegone bricklayer's insurance claim, damn near verbatim, from a post on the University of Vermont's ListServ that appeared in 1995, itself a retelling of a 1982 column printed in the *Louisville Courier-Journal*, performed earlier at the Oxford Union in 1958, not to mention Laurel & Hardy's take in the 1937 film *Way Out West*, and perhaps even—sources say—an article from as early as 1895, published in the *Cedar Rapids Evening Gazette*.

Normal, 2011

I donated the change from my purchase of *The Lost Steps* to a crappy shoebox with makeshift inscription for a "David Foster Wallace Memorial Fund," the validity of which I had first to check with the hipster kid behind the counter—this was back in 2011 after all—who assured me the Fund was "legit," and so left satisfied to crack open my new purchase and found that a previous owner had inscribed the first page with blue ink:

> , and some texts for music and ballet. In 1958 f short stories, *Guerra de Tempo* (*The War of* preparing a volume of stories inspired by the it about in Cuban society by the Revolution.
>
> *Deana Bartley*
> *Bermuda, 1971*

Bermuda, 1971

Three years after the island nation adopted a constitution and two years before its governor would be assassinated, I imagine Ms. Bartley's enjoyment, combing pink sand, inspecting shells' fractals, following Carpentier's unnamed narrator as he retreats deeper into the untamed tropics, Ms. Bartley herself a woman about whom no small amount of amateurish online research yielded very little information, the only potential lead a feature in the July 27th, 1971 edition of the *Milwaukee Sentinel*.

ONE OF THE NEW breed of young college professors is Mrs. Diana Bartley, director of an adult education institute for the teachers of inner city adults at the University of Wisconsin—Milwaukee. She is a careerist, wife, mother and community volunteer. —Sentinel Photo

Milwaukee, 1971

What began as a search for an answer to simple questions (Why Bermuda? Why Carpentier? Why in translation?), led me to Ms. Bartley's publishing record (extensive), employment history (respectable), linguistic proficiency and volunteer record (enviable, both), and ended with the portrait of an educator at the University of Wisconsin in a rather flattering profile, complete with quarter-page, B&W photograph.

New York, 1956

Despite her father's advice emphasizing "the education you will get and the contribution you will make to the world," at her social debut in Manhattan, an event designed basically to advertise the availability of her sex to men of standing, Ms. Bartley had "no hesitation whatever in putting her husband's career first," according to the *Sentinel*.

Caracas, 1956

Two years before the overthrow of its dictatorship, in a nation called "little Venice" by the navigator credited as the New World's namesake, I imagine Carpentier, the father of so-called magic realism, in exile from Cuba, his homeland, at the time, tracing his narrator's retreat into the jungle, his mad scramble to recover or constitute an identity, to identify with someone in this wild, only for Ms. Bartley before me to underline but one fragment of a single sentence in *The Lost Steps* I believe that we've shared:

> ...one said for a hidden or surprise meaning; I tried to catch them off guard with disconcerting, contradictory questions, but to no avail. My long experience in certain circles, my boasted sophistication, told me that I was behaving like a fool. And yet I was suffering something far worse than jealousy: the unbearable sensation of having been left out of a game that such omission made all the more hateful.
> I could not bear the perfidy, the hypocrisy, the mental picture conjured up of this hidden and pleasurable 'something' these women might be sharing behind my back...

New York, 2010

I'd like to think I know what Ms. Bartley meant by finding "something far worse than jealousy" worth underscoring, for in that same city where she made her social debut half a century earlier, I closed the back cover of *Oblivion*, having managed to consume the entirety of DFW's oeuvre, all of it, everything and more, mere days before I'd board a plane back to Evanston, Illinois, hours before I'd climb three flights of stairs to the Upper West Side apartment of the instructor who introduced me to him in the first place by announcing his death two years prior.

Evanston, 2009

Between my first and last years as a graduate student at Rutgers—The State University of New Jersey—I read contemporaneously with (but did not participate in) an annual estival group read of *Infinite Jest*, in which games feature as prevalently as addiction and entertainment and real human connectivity, such that my exclusion from it must have been my first move to shedding this anxiety of influence, the unbearable sensation of writing in the footsteps of a father.

Diego Báez
Chicago, 2014

"At the Very Terminus of His Tether": David Foster Wallace and the Situationist Ghost

Z. Bart Thornton

In a note near the end of *Infinite Jest* (1996), David Foster Wallace offers a sly allusion to the Situationist provocateur Guy Debord, who believed that true art was sparked by randomness and rupture. While watching *Blood Sister*, a film by the suicidal paterfamilias and avant-garde filmmaker James Orin Incandenza, a young tennis player/academician named Kent Blott demands a translation to an on-screen Latin caption. He is told the phrase means, "We Are What We Revile or We Are What We Scurry Around As Fast as Possible With Our Eyes Averted" (1054, n. 298). The self-consciously defeatist and clunkily prolix title recalls that of Debord's final film, *In girum nocte et consumimur igni [We Turn in the Night and Are Consumed by Fire]* (1978). For Wallace—whose knowledge of European cinema was vast,[1] if often diverted to parodic ends—the conjunctions between Debord's ideas and Incandenza's output are significant. The Debordian strategies of *dérive* (meaningful wandering) and *détournement* (cultural hijacking) are deeply embedded in Wallace's novel and JOI-wraith's frenetic movement through it.

Already, I must pause.

---

[1] Joelle van Dyne, Molly Notkin, and their film studies coterie share an evident fondness for European New Wave cinema ("like late Makavajev, something that's only entertaining after it's over, as reflection" [233]). In the Filmography, we're told that *Various Small Flames* mirrors "the neo-conceptualist structuralist films of *God*bout and Vodri*ard*" (988, n. 24); here, we see a not-so-veiled homage to Godard and his first film, *À bout de souffle* (1960).

Even the most hagiographical of Wallace's "fanboys" tend to take umbrage at the appearance of James Orin Incandenza's ghost. *Infinite Summer* stalwart Avery Edison claims that the wraith "doesn't so much *test* my suspension of disbelief as it does rip it apart and stomp on the broken remains while screaming, 'You're damn right there's ghosts now, Avery.'" Needless to say, I see the filmmaker's phantasm from a different vantage point. You'll recall that Don Gately—that "big indestructible moron" who's also in many ways the moral center of the novel—is in the hospital, eschewing Demerol, fading in and out of consciousness, when he detects "a tally insubstantial ghostish figure appearing and disappearing in the mist of his vision's periphery" (828). Although he initially assumes that this was one of his victims—in his previous incarnation, Gately was an addict, a burglar, a thug—he quickly concludes that the blur before him in a sweatshirt and chinos is merely "a garden-variety wraith" with a predilection for apologetic smiles and thin-shouldered shrugs (829). Let me cite a longer passage that will prove crucial to my argument:

> The wraith said[,] Even a garden-variety wraith could move at the speed of quanta and be anywhere anytime and hear *in symphonic toto* the thoughts of animate men, but…a wraith had no out-loud voice of its own, and had to use somebody's like internal brain-voice if it wanted to try to communicate something, which was why thoughts and insights that were coming from some wraith always just sound like your own thoughts, from inside your own head, if a wraith's trying to interface with you. (831; emphasis added)

Could it be that the "*symphonic toto*" of *Infinite Jest*—all those chattering voices—are being filtered through the spectral consciousness of the JOI-wraith as he passes (largely) invisibly through the discrete story arcs. After all, in life, The Mad Stork is a tennis prodigy turned optical scientist and avant-garde filmmaker who is a major political player in the ONAN reconfiguration *and* who is dogged by addiction and depression. All narrative lines pass through him. And in death, he gives voice to all the damaged, dispossessed, and downtrodden "figurants" (bit players) who inhabit Wallace's world. As the wraith looks pensively down at Gately, the latter flashes back to the show *Cheers*, "the nameless patrons always at tables,… concessions to realism, …always having silent conversations…; only the name-stars could audibilize" (834).[2] The JOI-wraith recognizes "what a miserable fucking bottom-rung job this must be for an actor" (834-835): being simultaneously present and absent.

Incandenza proceeds to explain that "in the entertainments [he] made,... he goddamn bloody well made sure that either the whole entertainment was silent or else...you could bloody well hear every single performer's voice, no matter how out on...the narrative periphery they were" (835). If you take Incandenza, at this moment at least, as an extension of Wallace, you understand why there are at least 200 characters *who matter* in this epic novel. Perhaps the most significant, and poignant, moment comes when "[t]he wraith blows his nose in a hankie that's...seen better epochs and says he, the wraith, when alive in the world of animate men, had seen his own personal youngest offspring, a son, the one most like him, the one most marvelous and frightening to him, becoming a figurant" (837). It's ironic that, as Incandenza channels the idiosyncratic voices and perspectives of 200-plus individuals, he loses the *specific sound* of his son. Clearly, JOI had been scarred by the "failure and self-loathing" (838) of his own father, whose drinking problem was on par with Incandenza's own. And, frightening him further, he had also seen evidence of Hal's fledgling addictive tendencies. The wraith eventually tells Gately that he "spent the whole sober last ninety days of his animate life working tirelessly to contrive a medium via which he and his son could simply *converse*....A way to say I AM SO VERY SORRY and have it heard" (838-839).³ Although apology was surely one of Incandenza's aims, he also wanted to reverse Hal's fall

---

² At least in my first-edition of *IJ*, George Wendt's beer-swilling curmudgeon is referred to not as "Norm" but as "Nom," which is, of course, the French word for "Name." If, as I think and hope, this is a deliberate misspelling on Wallace's part, we're being asked to think about the names of our odd couple: JOI, whose translated and pronounced initials speak ironically of mirth, and Gately, whose surname suggests a semi-restriction on a person's movement from one place to another. And the latter "nom" resonates with the proximal relationship that develops between Gately and "Madame Psychosis," whose own name alludes to the Greek word *metempsychosis*, the transmigration of the soul from one body to another (Burn, *David Foster Wallace* 61). She was there at the time of Gately's near-death, just as she was around at the time of Incandenza's slow-burn suicide.

³ At the end of the sequence, Gately shrewdly wonders why the wraith is wasting time with "some drug addict he doesn't know from a rock instead of just quantuming over to wherever this alleged youngest son is and...trying to have an interface with the fucking *son*" (840). By one interpretation, JOI-wraith is laying the foundation for Gately's subsequent relationship with Hal, one that moves from Ennet House rehab to the Quebec grave where, guarded by John "No Relation" Wayne, they will futilely attempt to retrieve the Entertainment from JOI's skull (16).

into a solipsism from which he would not escape.[4] It's a solipsism James Orin Incandeza knows all too well; even after absorbing and echoing the voices of hundreds, he cannot escape his own deeply suffused melancholy.

The film to which Incandenza refers is *Infinite Jest (V?)*, also known as *The Samizdat*. The last in a series of The Mad Stork's cinematic gambits, it is an entertainment so captivating it kills. The impossibly compelling film stands in stark contrast to some of his earlier, more ephemeral, "anti-art" efforts. After incurring critical wrath for *The Joke*—twin cameras projected the audience onto the screen as they grew increasingly "self-conscious, uncomfortable, and hostile" watching themselves (988, n. 24)—the filmmaker holed up at a detox facility in suburban Boston and "made up a genre that he considered the ultimate Neorealism,…Found Drama" (1027, n. 145). Academics hailed the new movement, which played out as another of Incandenza's pranks. He would tear a page out of a Boston phonebook and throw a dart at it from across the room. "And the name it hit [became] the subject of the Found Drama.…The joke's theory was that there's no audience and no stage or set because…in Reality there are none of these things. And the protagonist doesn't know he's the protagonist in a Found Drama because in reality nobody thinks they're in any sort of drama" (1027-1028, n. 145). Nothing is captured, nothing is filmed. The "artwork" remains a drunken gleam in the eye of its creator and a couple cronies.

The logic is positively Debordian. In 1950s Paris, Debord—a founder of The Lettrist International and the Situationist International—argued the world had seen enough *masterpieces*. "We care nothing," Debord wrote, "about the permanence of art or of anything else" ("Report" 41). In lieu of a "spectacular" culture rooted in consumption, he advocated for an art of impermanence and flux: defaced print ads, films without images, half-faked memoirs, sketches on cocktail napkins burned at the end of a bar-crawl. "Each day [the Situationists] would case the spectacles of art and

---

[4] The bond between Incandenza and Hal is subtly stressed throughout *Infinite Jest*. Here's one example. In the filmmaker's flashback of his father's disastrous mattress wrestling episode (Sepulveda, CA, B.S. 1963), we are *awash* in the color blue (494). The bed's sheets, pillowcases and coverlet, the room's carpeting and curtains and even its dust: all are blue. Hal's next section begins: "The following things in the room were blue" and proceeds through a cataloguing of "blue-family" items in the waiting room of his mother Avril's office (508). By my reading, this is a fairly clear example of JOI-wraith's communicating to his son through "ghost-words" and being heard and felt.

advertising, pillage bits and pieces, and make them speak in new tongues" (Marcus 163). At any rate, the process *always* superseded the product. Situationists must practice "[making] a passionate journey out of the ordinary through a rapid changing of ambiences" (Debord, "Report" 40). Debord's description aptly captures JOI-wraith's phantasmic amble through the tennis academy and halfway house, the silence of the Arizona desert where conspirators cavil, and the toxic Canadian landscape, overrun with feral hamsters and mutant children. It's hard to imagine more "rapid[ly] changing ambiences" than those we encounter in *Infinite Jest*.

"One day we'll build cities for drifting," Debord asserted (Hussey 105). Wallace's Boston is just that.[5] In two nocturnal ambles—one by Incandenza's muse, Joelle van Dyne, and one by the book's most repellent figure, Randy Lenz—we see two meaningfully disparate "drifts." Planning to die by overdose at her friend Molly Notkin's party, Joelle watches "the absolute end of her life and beauty running in a kind of stuttered old handheld 16mm before her eyes" and then recalls the walk she took from East Charles to the Back Bay in order to get to the soiree (221). Joelle notes a parallel between "the rain's wet veil" and her mentor's artistry: "Jim had designed his neonatal lens to blur things,…[a] blur more deforming than fuzzy" (222). Over the course of her cross-town walk, Joelle comes to understand the dimensions of her cage and sees herself, for better or worse, " in all four mirrors of her little room's walls" (223). If Debord argued only for the transcendent (and/or playful) qualities of the *dérive*, I would *hardly* be able to throw Lenz into the mix. In a grotesque sequence, the cocaine-addled rehab-imposter—who likes to go "abroad in the urban night, on almost a nightly basis, apparently strolling" (539)—finds and tortures a series of animals: rats, cats, and, finally, the Canadian dog whose poisoning leads to an increasingly calamitous series of events. *However*, in a dark light, Lenz, too, is an heir to the Situationists.

Debord claimed that "Situationist strategy would be an endless, ever-changing series of offensive actions…which would confuse and wrongfoot the enemy. 'We will wreck this world,' Debord claimed in an early manifesto" (Hussey 112). And Lenz does his damndest to do just that.

---

[5] In his introduction to *Signifying Rappers*, Mark Costello observes that Boston—through which he and Wallace wandered in the summer of 1989—is "topographically, a city of coves and necks, peninsulas and squares, an archipelago of many little inter-hostile hoods" (x).

Debord argued for a continual and "mutual interference of two worlds of feeling" (Debord and Wolman 15), an art rooted in juxtaposition, or *détournement*. Following the leads of such subversive theatrical writers/directors as Antonin Artaud and Bertolt Brecht, Debord contended that the "spectacle" should be defamiliarized and its foundations laid bare. Pre-existing elements—words, images, structures—should be hijacked and radically re-formed. In a world in which "Nothing works any more, and nothing is believed any more" (Hussey 365), all transformative tactics are fair game. These sentiments highlight the Situationists' debt to the Dada movement that preceded and influenced it. "In Paris, where so many of Dada's wandering emissaries returned after [World War I], a series of quasi-theatrical [events] seemed half celebration, half rebellious rebuff to the national 'return to order' that dominated Parisian postwar culture" (Dickerman 2). In Zurich, the artist Hans Arp

> made work by tearing paper into pieces, which he dropped to the floor pasted into place here they fell....[T]hese works introduced visual signs of disorder into the orderly system of the grid in the suggestion of random dispersal, the soft jagged edges of torn paper, and wobbling structures. (Dickerman 37)

Arp's technique, which capitalizes on randomness, recalls the Situationist tendency to roll a pair of dice to determine one's day. "[J]agged edges and wobbling structures": the description corresponds keenly to an image Wallace once used to describe his behemoth novel. "*Infinite Jest*," he told his friend Mark Caro, is like "a very pretty pane of glass…dropped off the twentieth story of a building" (Burn, *Conversations* xi).

"I will make no concessions to the public in the film." These are the first words Guy Debord speaks in his sixth and final film, *In girum imus nocte*. In the first few minutes—as the viewer takes in a static series of snapshots of dissatisfied consumers—Debord returns to some of the mantras he had been reciting at least since the publication of *The Society of the Spectacle* (1967). Those who control the modes of production, and shill its wares, have the rest of us "under constant petty surveillance." People "work overtime in the service of emptiness, and emptiness rewards them with coinage in its own image." And contemporary cinema is as corrupt as any other cultural mode; it offers little more than "a deranged imitation of a deranged life, a production skillfully designed to communicate nothing." Rather than provide the cheap narratives and camera tricks with which many filmmakers content themselves, Debord foregrounds the merits of his "recycling" project. "I pride myself," he says, "on having made a film out of whatever rubbish was at hand." But then, approximately midway through the film, Debord makes a curious swerve. "I am going to replace the frivolous adventures typically recounted by the cinema with the examination of an important subject: myself."

Let me swerve, back to the Filmography of James Orin Incandenza. In the most extensive end-note, the reader finds a preponderance of evidence that JOI is, like Debord, zeroing the camera in on himself. His films on junior tennis, annular fusion, and militant semanticists all directly accord with his lived experiences. Other movies, slightly more removed from Incandenza's daily existence, nevertheless correspond with his paranoia and fears: about adultery, spiders, dental work, and addiction. As the Filmography proceeds, chronologically, we see the increasingly intrusive presence of Death. Through his releases, the Mad Stork moves backward into his recollections of his own slurringly hard-driving father and forward into his prescient predictions about the world his sons will inhabit: a realm of catatonia, impossible yearning, and the heart-breaking nature of muteness. Despite his experimentalist trappings, Incandenza mined his own inescapable reality in order to concretize his larger aesthetic visions. In the years before his suicide, Incandenza's gaze becomes increasingly trained on Joelle van Dyne and death. These two have a close kinship. In *Mobius Strips*, a scientist "conceives of Death as a lethally beautiful woman" (990, n. 24); in *Low Temperature Physics*, a CEO becomes catatonic after "an ecstatic encounter with Death" (991); and, in *Infinite Jest*, Death is both a character in the film and an after-effect of viewing the film (993). In each case, Madame Psychosis *was* death.

In the hospital room, the wraith lets slip—and seep into Gately's addled brain—a series of "ghost-words" that constitute a kind of cryptic confession, or elusive autobiography. He speaks of the whirling and vertiginous sensations of a body in perpetual motion (*pirouette, proprioception*); such terms speak to his cycling through disparate careers, the alcoholic unsteadiness he experienced throughout his adult life, and his spectral swirlings. Incandenza alludes to his pioneering optical work (*neutral density point, chronaxy*) and his filmmaking pedigree (*chiaroscuro, bricolage*). And he reminds readers of his own father's beloved automobile, a *Cerise Montclair* that is at the center of an earlier flashback during which the washed-up actor Jim Incandenza tells his future filmmaking son that he should aspire to the condition of the car: "[Y]ou're a machine[,] an object, Jim, no less than this rutilant Montclair" (115). Why, though, does JOI-wraith feel the need to impart all of this to the convalescing Don Gately? If you accept the interpretation that Hal spends time in Gately's tutelage in the missing year between the Year of the Depend Adult Undergarment and the Year of Glad, you should also acknowledge that Gately should know as much as possible about the background of father and son. But there's also the matter of a single word. In a cogent explication, Jonathan Goodwin suggests that the key "ghost-word" might well be *luculus*, or "small box" (122). Goodwin posits that the word might refer to the container in which Incandenza's films are entombed in a Canadian field. He also pinpoints Lucullus, a Roman general who came to be known for his genius *and* his appetites. Cicero and Pompey were stunned by the lavish and wine-soaked banquets he would host. Upon hearing that Lucullus would have no guests for dinner, his steward brought him a rather unimpressive meal, only to be reprimanded: "Did you not know that tonight *Lucullus* dines with Lucullus?" *Infinite Jest* is a compendium of addictions and appetites, and in the allusion to Lucullus—for whom post-war life was a series of games—we see a reflection of both Incandenza and Debord: the brilliance, the egocentricity, and the wily, wily ways.

In the elegiac second half of *In girim*, Debord surveys his controversial career, confessing that he remains "completely incapable of imagining how he might have done anything any differently." Known for severing ties and burning bridges, Debord directly acknowledges his propensity for personal and professional rupture. Later, he asks what his counter-cultural strollings—full of "astonishing encounters, remarkable encounters, grandiose betrayals, perilous enchantments"—have really accomplished. But it is clear that Debord recognizes the merit of his own wanderings, which have provided him a way of accommodating the fallen world, a "wasteland where new sufferings are disguised with the name of former pleasures and where people are so afraid." On a cold November day in 1994, on his estate in Champot, Debord—suffering from alcoholic polyneuritis—shot himself in the heart. When I heard this news, four months out of graduate school, I couldn't help think of the final words Debord spoke in *In girim*, words that also recall the *wraithful* restlessness of James Orin Incandenza: "For me there will be no turning back and no reconciliation. No wising up and no settling down."

Works Cited

Burn, Stephen J., ed. *Conversations with David Foster Wallace*. Oxford: U of Mississippi P, 2012. Print.

—. *David Foster Wallace's* Infinite Jest, *A Reader's Guide*. 2nd ed. Bloomsbury Academic, 2012. E-book.

Debord, Guy. "Report on the Construction of Situations and on the International Situationist Tendency's Conditions or Organization and Action." [1957] Trans. Ken Knabb. *Bureau of Public Secrets*. 2006. Web. 22 February 2014.

In girim nocte consumimur igni. Dir. Guy Debord. 1978. Trans. Ken Knabb. *Bureau of Public Secrets*. 2003. Web. 1 March 2014.

Costello, Mark. "Introduction." *Signifying Rappers*. Boston: Little, Brown [1990], 2013. E-book.

Debord, Guy, and Gil J. Wolman. "A User's Guide to Détournement." [1956] Trans. Ken Knabb. *Bureau of Public Secrets*. 2006. Web. 14 February 2014.

Dickerman, Leah. *Dada: Zurich, Berlin, Hanover, Cologne, New York*. Washington, DC: The National Gallery of Art, 2005. Print.

Edison, Avery. "The Grapes of Wraith." *Infinite Summer*. 10 September 2009. Web. 17 March 2014.

Goodwin, Jonathan. "Wallace's *Infinite Jest*." *The Explicator* 61.2 (2003): 122-24. Print.

Hussey, Andrew. *The Game of War*. London: J. Cape, 2001. Print.

Marcus, Greil. *Lipstick Traces: A Secret History of the Twentieth Century*. 2nd ed. Cambridge: Belknap/Harvard UP, 2009. Print.

Wallace, David Foster. *Infinite Jest*. Boston: Little, Brown, 1996. Print.

—, and Mark Costello. *Signifying Rappers*. Little, Brown [1990], 2013. E-book.

Lisa Is the Water

JoAnna Novak

"The worst toy for a bulimic is a garbage disposal," you say.

Saturday afternoon on the balcony, flattened out in bikinis with pink rosettes kissing the waist, glasses of Perrier and a bowl of limes on the towel between you and Lisa. Summer physics ended yesterday, and you've been fasting since the final to be angles and elbows for back-to-school.

Lisa flips. Her blonde hair drips down her back and her shoulder blades jut like wings.

"No way," Lisa says. "All-you-can-eat buffet."

"You're cliché," you say. "Everyone says that."

"Who's everyone?"

"Every girl in every hospital." You think Lisa may be getting a little dippy, to lift one of your mother's favorites. All that time she's spending with Chris: Semen kills brain cells. You're a little light-headed evaluating the situation through sunglasses, trying to clench your transverse abdominals, peeved, like when you clogged the drain in the bathtub and needed to pour a whole Drano down and didn't want to call your father to get the window—that was last month. Always with those windows that stick. Why are they so hard to open?

The fast is new; the summer, the same. You and Lisa have committed to summer school to rid yourselves of requirements, but you've never seen Lisa let a boy eat up so much of her time. Before you were high schoolers, you sat next to each other in a chilly lab relearning home row and business letter blocks. And chemistry: you burned peanuts and calculated a calorie—nothing but energy enough to heat one measly gram of water.

Now you picture yourself in the white lab coat you borrowed from the teacher every day; that summer you were so cold you called your hands prayer candles.

Mottled, lit, blue.

Half a day you laze away while maintenance buzzes below. Big green trucks from Crown Disposal stink gasoline across the lawn and snatch grass from the cul-de-sac; men prune and trim, roses and hedges. Beneath your balcony, a crew of gray jumpsuits tends to a bed of impatiens with handhelds like weaponry, engines revving—eight men, burnished and sweating.

"I think we should be done," you say. "I'm really…from the sun." At the gym, you almost passed out during spinal imprints. Long legs, the instructor crowed through her puffy bangs. Remember your powerhouse, ladies. Pilates is what stays still!

"Dizzy."

"You don't feel good? I feel totally good, just like…chill," Lisa says. She props herself on her elbows, wipes a hair from her forehead. Picks up a lime and dunks it in her sparkling water. Sucking the fruit lights her eyes. "Mmm, do this. Fizzy."

You glare at your watch.

"We're not eating until five." You move the band up your elbow and lust on the bracelet of pale flesh, the brindle brown hair sweat-plastered. If you were alone, you'd nose the skin, inhale animal and wood chips and sun. "It's quarter after two."

Your body leaves a long, dark oval on the towel when you sit and reach for your robe. Coward. Viscera of soul. You avoid your stomach: bending forward or reaching down or craning for the alarm or right after you've eaten—fine, all food bloats your belly just the same; sometimes, you stare yourself down in the mirror and think, you'd be fine—for a pregnant bitch.

"It's a lime," Lisa says. She cracks her neck. Tendons, striae, pretty, slack.

"Ten calories."

You stare. Lower your voice: "So, what else doesn't count?"

Lisa's face shrinks, a sucked-out prune. "Nothing, nothing else—all right? Re-lax. I just think, the point of the fast is to not eat. A lime's not really eating."

"I'd say ten calories is like…eating," you say.

Mocking you learned from your mother. Smog in air. Nothing but summer. It's you and Lisa. So Lisa's not your best friend anymore, no problem. Maybe, she can collect your assignments when you head back to the hospital.

"It doesn't matter," you say. You imagine displacing the blood racing through your body with bubbling water until you feel nothing, maybe benevolent, mostly dizzy. Breathe: let your blood pressure tumble. Out: wafting neuro-trauma. No one's making you eat a stupid lime.

#

Lisa slips into the bedroom, past your vanity, all clothing and charts, your diaries, one for tracking and another, blank, waiting for recovery to clutch your stupid shoulders and douse you with fat, and Lisa grabs her clothes from the back of a chair and disappears into the bathroom to change while you wait.

You're alone in your bedroom. You're so ethereal from fasting you want to wear something with a skirt to usher air in and out, but all your dresses look like they're waiting for someone else. A silhouette better than you.

Lisa.

Reframe, Reframe, Reframe—so, okay, maybe there's no such thing as better.

Loose in the bust, looser in the hips, scoop-necked and white. Who will judge if your swimsuit shows through? You're your only judge. The halter brands your neck, a floppy bow tipped with shiny gold charms.

You sit on your bed and stare at the television, mute. Scoot to the edge. A million music video countdowns, junkfood and trash. No wonder your parents tried the cable ban: Kurt Cobain is lambent, cheerleaders' braids are swinging; a crowd swells, a janitor mopes with his bucket.

"Wanna go to the mall?" you say.

You picture Lisa on the other side of the door.

Legs: scalpels, ice picks, bone. Bone and more bone, nuzzled under Lisa's golden, sun-kissed flesh. Nothing hungry in her eyes. Breasts: plump. Bouncy, even. What would she do with your mouth?

"The mall is freezing."

"It's like a hundred degrees out," you say, swiping a finger behind your knee where sweat gathers in a thin stripe like the moistened seal of an envelope. Barely a secret. You're overheating and Lisa's freezing?

No way Lisa is thinner.

"I'm sick of shopping," Lisa says. "Let's go to the V."

#

You don't just suspect this has a lot to do with Chris; the V means Chris, head lifeguard who keeps Lisa at the pool late, way after close, to kiss her long, ballerina neck beneath a sky blistered with stars. This is your favorite way to think of Lisa—though you've heard about hot tub parties, flirty drinking games and fingerprint bruises—no, not jealously. Envy you buy at a counter. Lisa's always inviting you, calling you, offering to pick you up or bring you out, but you're convinced your parents just pay Lisa to help you maintain normal teenage life—like they know you that well, like they get that you'd rather be studying your ascetic saints than cruising the cul-de-sac with Lisa; that, every night, you wrestle yourself into believing that God will cradle your consciousness like a worry stone when you finally win, with a clavicle gnash and your pulse's ultimate curlicue, when you wear your body down.

#

The matching halter strap around Lisa's neck? One velum valentine after another floats through your body, your heart shaved on a mandoline. Your breath quickens, your stomach growls: inside, another continent, where everything graspable drowns.

Lisa stops a foot from the television and gapes. Kurt Cobain's twiny hair slaps his forehead; her face is still pink-blushed, flushed.

"He was so hot—so hot, such a freak…"

"Where are we going?" you say.

Stanch your want with gravel, sand, clay, dirt.

"The V, yeah? Chris is working." She pulls her pinky across her teeth. "We get stuff free."

#

Lisa drives to the pool listening to a station playing upbeat pop. Top down, windows down, air conditioning blasting your feet. Pool bags in the backseat. In yours—towel, sun block, a roll of Necco wafers to ease you from the fast. What's inside Lisa's tote?

You look at your nails, try to rename the polish. Appointments. You have these. You have, also, a manicurist. Trainer, nutritionist, doctor, shrink. Who else do you see other than Lisa and your parents, the cook and the landscapers, the men who occupy the gatehouse? When was the last time you even went to the pool? All you remember is your final summer with the diving team, a few months before your twelfth birthday—normal as ever, when you did a one-and-a-half and slammed into the ice-blue board. Three rectangular gouges: forehead, chin, the bridge of your nose.

Charred meat and lilacs. Suburban trap of traffic and stop signs. Lisa sings along to every single song and some jingles. When the light turns red, Lisa stops too close. You turn into your mother: gasp and shrink, pump an imaginary brake. And if there's a man in the car on Lisa's side, she lowers her heart-shaped sunglasses and looks. Bats her eyes, licks her lips, hi.

"You do it," she says. "C'mon."

"I'm not flirting with some old man, Lisa."

"Make his dreams come true," she says. "Every father wants a sixteen-year-old."

"Sick," you say. "Nausea."

Three dreams. Your father: dead; your mother: banished. You unbuckle your nerdy chemistry teacher's belt with your teeth. Wake up and wait for your wanting to quit.

"Okay, look," Lisa says. "Red bug, on your right." She glances and, from behind your glasses, you follow her eyes. He's wearing a white tank-top and aviators, gold. "Oh my god, those arms."

"Are you hungry?" you say. Lamb-spit arms. Chainsaw guns.

"No. Remember? That lime? Kidding."

"No," you say. He's drumming the steering wheel to the dance music blaring and you wish you could apologize for catching him in such a pathetic pose.

"Seriously, if you don't, I will," Lisa says.

"Do it," Lisa says. Sun sparks her lips. Her mouth is one fat wish. "The light's about to change."

"No."

Lisa cranks the radio and he turns. "Now!"

You don't think. You pivot in your seat, little smile, wave. His eyebrows appear over the top of his glasses. He grins: perfect canines.

And green, zoom, onward, he's gone.

Lisa eyes you, her mouth open wide—a gob of neon gum and her silver filling (second molar, lower left). She laughs and throws her hands up, accelerating past the park district.

"Now, what about that was so bad?"

#

By the time you reach the pool, you're picking off your polish. Trying to fleck it between the door and the seat. There's not much to get excited about when therapy teaches you how to manage all your epiphanies. And Lisa gets out of the car, yawns, and stretches her long thin arms above her head. You've never seen any drastic weight changes—in fact, Lisa's always been slender—now she's just grown into it like a starlet—and, here she is, fasting for fun. Poor Lisa, you think. She got gorgeous, she got lazy.

"What are you going to eat first?" Lisa crouches, reapplying her lip gloss and pouting in the side mirror. "I feel so gross, but I know I want a pretzel. Or, like, frozen pizza—you know? Or, sickest—oh, I'm nasty: Chris has me hooked on churros in cheese."

Your decision is instant.

"I'm extending," you say. Catherine of Siena ate flesh and herbs; Beatrice bound herself with cords. For the first time in weeks, you feel your devotion, ticking.

"Till tomorrow."

"I don't really think that's a good idea…" Lisa says, but you're already walking to the gate.

The V is tucked away by a grove of weeping willows. The parking lot is a wash of gravel, a couple basketball hoops near the fence that wraps around the pool. A picnic pavilion with benches and grills, a bulletin board behind glass where swim practice schedules are posted along with Swimmers of the Week. From the lot, you hear screams, splashing, music tinny over the loudspeaker—everything in the distance glistening and candy. As you walk, small stones crack like teeth against the soles of your sandals.

Lisa jogs over in her sequined flip-flops, her tote banging against her hip, electric tangerine. Is the rubber strap digging pink into her shoulder? Water, aloe, neon gel: a salve for any sore. She catches up with you before the locker room.

"Would you wait, or are you going to be a bitch the rest of the day?"

"I'm not a bitch," you say, letting your own bag dangle off your wrist. You put your hand on your hip, thumb the bone, breathe in, glance at Lisa and look down. You've gotten good at shaking away her face.

"How am I a bitch?"

Two boys in saggy trunks and mesh water shoes tear past, through the beds of red geraniums that line the sidewalk up to the front desk. "You're it," one of them screams, pointing at you and jogging backwards before he disappears.

"Hon," Lisa says. "Can I give you a hug?"

Brace yourself. Hugs happen whether you like them or not. Lisa's a few inches taller than you and when she hugs you it's not two clanging skeletons—Lisa's breasts press into your chest. Things you don't have. Her hands rub your back. Hip bones, spine, the fine hairs glistening above her lip. You're drowsy off contact.

Up close, Lisa smells like ice cream, coconut.

Up close, you peer, finally, into her bag: towel; lightweight novel; a bag of pink-frosted animal crackers; a blue condom wrapper.

You pull away, tuck your hair behind your ears, stare hard and try to say something, not just anything.

"It's not good to full-on fast," Lisa says. "You told me that."

"I know."

"So, stop at five. Like the plan."

"I don't really want to," you say, licking your lower lip, tasting your skin, dark as blood blisters.

"Chris will give us food. At least get a diet Coke."

"I'm fine. I just need a swim."

#

You take five minutes peeing so you don't have to rinse off in the communal shower. You've seen it before: water beads Lisa's forehead like a veil, the drops cling to Lisa's nose like fleet piercings. When you're sure she's gone, you're alone in the steam. There are no mirrors, no curtains, no cover for tears. The water pelts your back. The floor tires your feet.

Lisa is on deck, beneath the guard's chair where Chris scans the diving well. Chris can give her food. Lisa is so aimless; Lisa needs to eat. You settle between a woman asleep in a black one-piece and an old man with breasts like soft triangles. You spread your towel out and sit down; you rifle through your bag until you find sun block. From here, Chris is a bright blue nose and sunglasses, tousled honey hair and a runner's concave chest. Rarely do you admit to yourself: you're so hungry that you're not. You're so hungry that, when you rest a hand on the slats of the chair, you watch your fingers float off, one by one, lifting toward Lisa. And Chris is twirling his whistle. Chris, who feeds her. And the woman in the black suit snores. The old man clears his throat. You squirt lotion onto your palm and feel your face. Ridge of nose, plum-skin eyes, stupid mouth. The line up the high dive is deep.

#

When will you find yourself at the V again?

Each summer will be less-Lisa than the last.

Each summer: another step away from turning back.

Two more summers: independence. The freedom of choosing when and how to end.

#

Your turn to climb the ladder. You grip each rung tight, and just feel, just deal, bear it, it makes you want to vomit: the sloughed-off skin of other people's feet, the moisture clinging to the metal, and then, at the top, that dirty plank. So you think, okay, two minutes, give yourself two minutes because bodies have amassed, queued, and you're not even nearing the edge. Just think about it. Just think. Just your friend and a thin slice of skin on her back, what the strap leaves light, and the rest of her body—soft caramel—and the tuft of hair between her legs sequined with saliva, so it's Lisa and Lisa, just Lisa. Lisa in the water, Lisa in the kiddie pool, Lisa inflating dolphins, Lisa your flotation device, Lisa licking, it's too slippery, Lisa saying well yah I said yea when he, as in ohyea, like ohyesbaby, Lisa in a car pinkying Xs and Os, Lisa as your mirror, Lisa's hands and knees—, it's no biggie, whatever, Lisa in the shower, Lisa skipping class, Lisa in the hot tub in her basement, above ground in the dark, Lisa and the Coke can, Lisa and the lights, all night Lisa, and the handcuffs tight, Lisa and the what, so I liked it, Lisa and donuts or batteries, melon!, Lisa drinking tons of water and fuck, nails Pacific Blue, picking out a pearl thong, purchasing the Pleasure Pack, Lisa in the future, Lisa with a football player, Lisa horizontal, Lisa saying multiple, we're talking three or four, holy holy fuck, Lisa Jesus Christing through getting eaten out, Lisa and her ankles, Lisa to the wall, Lisa on all fours, Lisa on her back on her front with her legs straight in a V two fingers on her lips with her tongue touching her chin with her eyelashes with her hair with her stomach sticky and flattened and toned and teased: parenthesis.

The whistle blows.

Chris points from his perch. His neck is bruised with Lisa.

He lifts his sunglasses. He squints. You hate him. You hate Chris-plus-Lisa, and you hate Lisa: next to Lisa, you're nothing.

Inhale and swallow. Your saliva tastes like beeswax. You turn around. Walking off means backing down the ladder or a peerless concrete drop. Your heart's pounding, your stomach's stinging; you grip the rails and feel for the rung, your gut level with the board.

And you smell her: Coconut. Sun-soaked hair. Candy-sweet wrists.

"Babe," Lisa calls.

You look down: nothing but Lisa, kiss-pink lips eating up the sun.

"Lisa Is the Water" was first published in Joyland

'Radically antifundamentalist': Notes Toward a Post-Secular Poetic in David Foster Wallace

Shannon Minifie

I. Being Ironic While Talking About Religion

Wallace once described his writing as an attempt to use "postmodern formal techniques for very traditional ends,"[1] and while Wallace's penchant for self-reflexive irony has remained at the forefront of critical discussions about the late writer,[2] considerably less attention is paid to the complicated relationship between his persistent use of irony and the nature of these so-called "traditional" ends. Setting aside the notion of irony as a strictly postmodern inheritance, this paper takes up the complicated nature of those "ends," considering Wallace's apparent commitment to irony in relation to the many post-secular themes in some of his work. It is my contention that the emergent interdisciplinary discourse of post-secularism not only provides a useful and refreshing lens for thinking about Wallace's preoccupation with religious belief, but also intersects in interesting and potentially fruitful ways with many conceptualizations of irony. Wallace's critique of irony in "E Unibus Pluram" and elsewhere is well known, so

---

[1] Interview in Capri, Italy. "Le Conversazioni." 2006. YouTube.
[2] And more recently, the focus has been on his apparent disdain for irony, and return to a (new) sincerity (see Adam Kelly, "David Foster Wallace and the New Sincerity in American Fiction" in *Consider David Foster Wallace*. Ed. David Hering, Los Angeles: Slideshow Media Group Press, 2010. 131-146. See also Mary K. Holland, "Mediated Immediacy in *Brief Interviews with Hideous Men*" in *A Companion to David Foster Wallace Studies*. Eds. Marshall Boswell and Stephen J. Burn. New York: Palgrave MacMillan, 2013. 107-130; and Lee Konstantinou, "No Bull: David Foster Wallace and Postironic Belief" in *The Legacy of David Foster Wallace*. Eds. Samuel Cohen and Lee Konstantinou. Iowa City: University of Iowa Press, 2012. 83-112).

I won't rehearse it here.³ We might recall, though, that in what has now become a familiar move, Wallace pits irony and conviction, suggesting that the irreverence of irony is antithetical to the sincerity of irony's ostensible opposite: principled conviction.

While many critics seem to agree with Wallace's dichotomy, accepting that irony is incompatible with sincerity or earnestness,⁴ Brad Frazier resists this oppositional conception of irony and conviction, pointing out that we "commonly seek in our lives … a mean between *unreflective devotion* and *hypercritical disengagement*,"⁵ and suggesting that this "mean" may be found in particular conceptions of irony. Jonathan Lear⁶ similarly considers irony as a middle place between these two extremes, and (following Kierkegaard), conceives of irony not as a mere verbal trick, but as an *experience* and *way of living*. Lear writes that "[w]e tend to think casually of 'the ironist' as someone who is able to make certain forms of witty remarks, perhaps saying the opposite of what he means, of remaining detached by undercutting any manifestation of seriousness;" however, the "deeper form of ironist," Lear explains, "is one who has the capacity to occasion an experience of irony."⁷ Basic to all irony is the discrepancy between appearance and reality, but the ironic experience as Lear describes it is a moment when we realize – are indeed *frozen by*—the discrepancy between what appears to be and what might be, in 'reality.' Lear's sense of irony is thus informed by the conception of humanity as a "task," or in other words, the notion that "being human involves living up to an ideal,"⁸ and he explains that it is this tendency to live in the shadows of our ideals that "set[s] us up for the [ironic] fall," which "can occur when the pretense simultaneously expresses and falls short of its own aspiration;" thus, irony, rather than a desire to deflect meaning or convey a humorous

---

³ And for an excellent discussion of the ways in which that critique has been misunderstood, see Allard den Dulk, "Beyond Endless Aesthetic Irony: A Comparison of the Irony Critique of Soren Kierkegaard and David Foster Wallace." Studies in the Novel. 44.3 (2012): 325-345.
⁴ Again, see Kelly, Holland and Konstantinou (above).
⁵ *Rorty and Kierkegaard on Irony and Moral Commitment*. New York: Palgrave MacMillan, 2006. 1. Emphases mine.
⁶ *A Case For Irony*. Cambridge: Harvard UP, 2011.
⁷ Lear 9.
⁸ What Lear calls the capacity for and practice of "pretense," something he argues is crucially a *human* practice integral to our sense of identity and our orientation in the world. His debts to Kierkegaard are clear here as well.

inside joke, is more properly understood as "the activity of bringing this falling short to light *in a way that is meant to grab us*."[9] Thus ironic *existence* would describe a life that continually acknowledges this gap between our pretenses and the idea(l)s on which that "pretending" is modeled. It is a continual disruption and re-working of what we think we know about our self and the world.

Post-secular thinkers seem similarly interested in navigating a middle course between earnest belief and hyper-critical skepticism at a time when belief in objective truth has become impossible. John McClure[10] has recently demanded the rethinking of dominant characterizations of "the postmodern period and the cultural produces identified with it as thoroughly and satisfactorily secularized,"[11] challenging these secular theoretical frameworks by pointing to postmodern fictions in which characters "insistently interrogate secular conceptions of the real," negotiating a "middle position" between "belief" and "unbelief" in narratives that are characterized by the *simultaneous espousal and disavowal* of religious beliefs which have been "dramatically 'weakened'" or delinked from authoritative and absolutist sources.[12] McClure calls these narratives "post-secular fictions," and he sees Italian philosopher Gianni Vattimo's notion of "weak thought" as key to these expressions of post-secularity, arguing that these writers are similarly engaged in navigating the post-metaphysical space between the postmodernists' critiques of secular certainty and the "secular critiques of traditional religion."[13] What Vattimo calls "weak thought" is in practice a hedge against nihilism and relativism: in the place of "objective" truth, Vattimo posits the interpretation of narratives that—while historically contingent and therefore lacking metaphysical certainty—nevertheless structure our experience and provide a foundation for the values and beliefs that lend coherence to our lives and identities. This kind of thinking, this form of belief, is "weak" precisely because it acknowledges its own provisionality and contingency, waiting for others to propose a more

---

[9] Lear 13.
[10] In two companion pieces, "Postmodern/Post-Secular: Contemporary Fiction and Spirituality" (*Modern Fiction Studies*. 41.1 (1995): 141-63), and "Post-Secular Culture: The Return of Religion in Contemporary Theory and Literature" (*Cross Currents*. (Fall 1997): 332-47), and in a monograph, *Partial Faiths: Post-Secular Fiction in the Age of Pynchon and Morrison* (Athens: University of Georgia Press, 2007).
[11] McClure (1995) 141-2.
[12] McClure (2007)142.
[13] McClure (2007)142.

plausible alternative. As Jeffrey Robbins explains, "this weak ontology also weakens the strong metaphysical reasons for atheism and the rationalist repudiations of religion…Now that we live in the postmetaphysical age in which there are no absolute truths, *only interpretations*, the category of belief can again be taken seriously as constitutive of our lived traditions."[14]

Graham Huggan similarly describes post-secular positions as "radically antifundamentalist…articulat[ing] the avoidance of *both* the extremes of dogmatic religion and the equally dangerous hyper-rationalist convictions of the so-called secular mind."[15] Maintaining an ambivalent position toward the "strong" beliefs of religious orthodoxy and dogma, while tending toward a "weak" or "partial" faith, much of Wallace's work expresses the liminality that is characteristic of post-secular thinking, as his characters attempt to navigate a middle course between credulity and skepticism, desiring a way to ground meaning and justify commitments. My contention is that, in Wallace's work, the function and effect of irony frequently intersect with both the philosophical possibilities and the practical consequences of post-secular thinking. Thus, I want to consider whether *irony* may be particularly useful for expressing Wallace's "post-secular" "mean": an in-between mode and destabilizing force, irony aligns itself with the liminality and provisionality of the post-secular "middle" course. Thus, irony, as a kind of poetic of in-betweenness, rather than undermining Wallace's expression of religious commitment, may prove to be a singularly useful post-secular poetic.

II. "All That"

One such "in-between" position may be found in the uncertain faith of the narrator of a short fragment of Wallace's, titled "All That" when it appeared in the *New Yorker* in 2009.[16] The story is an "uncomfortable" believers' recollection of a series of childhood experiences that he claims as the origins of his "lifelong religious feeling." The narrator recalls the way in which a cement mixer he received for Christmas as a small child became the catalyst for this religious impulse after his parents tell him that the mixer has "magical properties," casually convincing him that the cement mixer's drum rotates when—and *only* when—he is not looking.

---

[14] Robbins, Jeffrey W. *After the Death of God*. New York: Columbia UP, 2007. 16-17.
[15] Huggan, Graham. "Is the 'Post' in 'Postsecular' the 'Post' in 'Postcolonial'?" *Modern Fiction Studies*. 56.4 (2010): 751-768. 754.
[16] Wallace, David Foster. "All That." The *New Yorker*. 14 December 2009. Web.

While the child's naïveté seems quaint—he describes the various strategies he deployed in attempts to "catch the magic"—this marked lack of skepticism is clearly valorized over the "ad-hoc intellectual mania for empirical verification" that characterizes the narrator's parents who "cannot imagine doubt's complete absence." The narrator admits that "it never occurred to [*him*] to doubt," as his attempts to see the rotating mixer are motivated less by a desire to "catch" the magic, as to *confirm* it, since, he admits: "[i]f I had ever been successful in outsmarting the magic, I would have been crushed. I know this now."

The narrator reveals that this budding "religious interest" was *also* linked to his childhood tendency to "hear voices," voices that "appeared to *him*" as "entirely real and autonomous phenomena." He admits that "the ecstatic feelings [the voices] often aroused doubtless contributed to [his] reverence for magic," and his description of the "voices" as "*both real but* unobservable and unexplainable," collapses the binary distinctions that police the secular "real." He is anxious to verify the 'reality' of these voices, yet also willing to remain in a liminal place where the "voices" are neither empirically verified nor explicitly ascribed to a divinity. The final "traceable origin" of his "religious impulse" is the narrator's memory of a war movie he watched on television with his father. The narrator's recollection of this movie's "hero" is markedly different from his father's memory and stages the subjective nature of individual interpretation while reflecting the moral framework out of which the narrator is now, apparently, writing. His memory of the movie's "war hero" hinges on his interpretation of the lieutenant's act as one of self-sacrificial love for his enemies—a moral principle that is rife with Christian connotations. What the narrator seems to connect with his "religious impulse" here is his own sense of what constitutes "heroic" *character*, and that is something that is rooted in values and beliefs whose validity and source the narrator is apparently still unsure of, even as he betrays a kind of fidelity to them.

In this brief story, then, secular and religious intuitions battle generationally (the child vs. the parents), as well as within the narrator, who is, finally, a rather undecided "convert," one who we might say possesses "partial faith." The narrator's "weakened" relationship to this divine presence—one he never names or connects to any kind of dogma—is one that hinges crucially on the liminal, uncertain quality of post-secular belief. And these two impulses also battle structurally: the story exploits the split between the child and the adult narrator quite heavily in a typically ironic structure that juxtaposes precisely what I see as characteristic of post-secularity and irony, namely, this space between naïvete and skepticism. Speaking of the final "origin" of his religious feeling, the narrator asserts that he "never forgot the movie…or the impact of the lieutenant's act, which, I…regarded as not only heroic but also beautiful in a way that was almost too intense to bear." Here, the power of remembrance helps to bridge skepticism and naïvete, providing perhaps the only sense of conclusion in the story, which ends mid-rumination.

I want to argue that despite the *many* ironic elements—the *preciousness* of the child's recollections; the juxtapositions between the cement mixer and the mystery of a divinity; the stereotypical implications of "hearing voices;" the structural irony of the child/adult narrator – the story does not seem to undermine or negate the value of religious belief; but rather, it invites us to consider the highly subjective and perhaps uniquely difficult nature of trying to express spiritual commitments, thus opening up a space for our own thoughtful reflection. The irony here does not simply suggest that this narrator continues to be naively "duped" into believing in "magic;" instead, the irony seems to destabilize or inject doubt into *all* positions expressed in the story, "atheist" and "religious" alike. The kind of all-pervasive irony we may have here makes it understandably difficult to "reconstruct" the 'real' (or "stable") ironic meaning. The presence of irony also injects a kind of *ambiguity* into the text. It is due to this ambivalence, this negotiation of the middle ground, that Lillian Furst characterizes irony as "an inquiring mode that exploits discrepancies, challenges assumptions…but that does not presume to hold out answers."[17] It seems significant, then, that this story does not "hold out" any answers – it is concerned chiefly with the process of working through the grounds and plausibility of the narrator's commitments.

III. "Good People"

Wallace similarly visits the grounds for moral commitment in another fragment, collected in *The Pale King*, but excerpted earlier as a story titled "Good People."[18] In the story, Lane Dean, Jr., through whom the fragment is closely focalized, and his girlfriend have gathered at a picnic table to discuss their difficult decision to abort an unplanned pregnancy. They

---

[17] Furst, Lillian R. *Fictions of Romantic Irony*. Cambridge: Harvard UP, 1984. 9.
[18] In The *New Yorker*, 7 February 2007. Web.

both assume prayerful postures, with their "shoulders rounded and elbows on their knees" (1), and the girlfriend even "rock[s] slightly...but she was not crying" (1). The girlfriend, figured as the more confident Christian of the pair, is silently and stoically meditative. Lane, our troubled believer, is on the other hand, "very still and immobile" as he struggles to stay "sharp and alert" as he does "[s]ometimes when alone and thinking or struggling to turn a matter over to Jesus Christ in prayer."[19] (1). His insecurity, his unsureness of his own faith and his own *ability to pray* for help in the face of this problem paralyzes him, and he admits that "[t]he worse he felt, the stiller he sat.... He hated himself for sitting so frozen."[20] Lane is "frozen" because he is caught between what he is, in reality, and what he has appeared or aspired to be. His internal struggle between what he *wants* (for his girlfriend to have the abortion) in the face of what, through his Christian view of morality, he feels is *required* of him in order to be "good," is the central conflict of the story. Lane admits that he knows the right answer to their problem—he should tell his girlfriend that he loves her, so that she will keep the baby and not the appointment—but he also admits that his "hypocritical" behaviour is motivated by his efforts to avoid asking for help through prayer, since he senses the gap between his own desires and what he says he knows to be "right." This, he realizes, "might be the frozen resistance - were he to look right at her and tell her he didn't [love her], she would keep the appointment and go."[21] And this is why he cannot pray: because he is divided within himself, lying to himself while still trying, half-heartedly, to be "good" and do the "right" thing; he admits that "[h]e was starting to believe that he might not be serious in his faith. He was desperate to be good people, to still be able to feel he was good."[22]

Despite his reluctance to pray, Lane's ruminations and doubts prove to be a form of prayer themselves, as he has what he calls a "moment of vision," as he suddenly becomes aware of his own humanity: "[h]e was not a hypocrite, just broken and split off like all men. Later on, he believed that what happened was he'd had a moment of almost seeing them both as Jesus saw them, as blind but groping, wanting to please God despite their inborn fallen nature."[23] This epiphany also enlightens him that Sheri will

---

[19] Wallace, David Foster. *The Pale King*. 37.
[20] Ibid.
[21] Wallace 40.
[22] Wallace 39.
[23] Wallace 42.

go on to tell him she cannot go through with the abortion, but will carry the child to term—on her own—because "this is what love commands of her."[24] Like "All That," this story ends without the finality of a choice, but the questions Lane confronts in his "vision" are the occasion for critical reflection on his beliefs—reflection that, the final lines suggest, helps to confirm his commitment to them. Lane asks himself: "Why is he so sure he doesn't love [Sheri]? Why is one kind of love any different? What if he has no earthly idea what love is? What would even Jesus do?"[25]

As elsewhere in Wallace's work, there is a preponderance of spiritual- or religious-type diction, reference, and allusion; however, Lane's reassessment of his "personal relationship with Jesus Christ" (once again staged as a kind of "crisis of faith") seems also to be an occasion for the "experience of irony," one in which, Lear explains, "[i]t is as though an abyss opens between our previous understanding and our dawning sense of an ideal to which we take ourselves already to be committed."[26] In this particular moment of irony, what Lear characterizes as an "occasion for disruption and disorientation,"[27] Lane's convictions—so centrally constitutive of his character up to this point—are called into question as he faces a disparity between his sense of identity and the ideal to which he aspires: the series of questions that comprise his epiphany force him to re-assess the vocabulary that undergirds his values, and as he faces the limits of his own understanding, he finally considers that his idea(l) of love might be far away from "what love is." This question, "What would even Jesus do?" defamiliarizes what, for Lane, would be an all-too-familiar platitude, but Lane interrogates what has basically become a cliché, demanding that the question once again be taken seriously: the question "what would even Jesus do?" interrogates what it might *actually* mean to try to live up to the ideal.

IV. Concluding

I want to suggest that we might consider these characters' crises of faith as exemplary instances in which the experience of irony—that critical reflection on one's identity and ideals—requires them to revisit the grounds for their beliefs in order that they might renew their commitment to them.

---

[24] Ibid.
[25] Wallace 43.
[26] Lear 15.
[27] Lear 14.

But more than a mode of critical reflection, irony is also a very good distancing tool. And we might very well read these stories as examples of the very "ironic distance from deep convictions and desperate questions" which Wallace himself lamented. In Lane's story, we might read that little word, "even," as an authorial intrusion of sorts, a moment when the narrative, focalized through Lane, floats ever so slightly in the direction of the narrator, whom we might imagine to be some version of Wallace himself. Read this way, "What would *even* Jesus do" is the narrator's sly wink to the reader, an eye-roll, a moment when this character, and his stereotypical phrase, is being ironized. This use of irony as a "protective garment" might be just what Wallace needed in what he perceived to be an environment of "congenital skepticism,"[28] a literary community suspicious of all conviction, averse to the "banal" topic of religious belief: a way for Wallace to distance himself from the very ideas with which his characters are engaged.

Rather than chalking up Wallace's tendency to irony as evidence of his own work's immersion in the context of "institutionalized irony," what if we considered the positive aspects of irony, especially for the post-secularist? What if, rather than ironizing Lane Dean Jr.'s struggle to be "good," or mocking the credulous, childlike experience of the narrator in "All That," we consider why it is that we refuse to accept things at face value? Why we, ourselves, insist on being "perfectly sure"? Because perhaps this "ironic" distance is rather more like the kind of irony Lear has in mind. Linda Hutcheon, for instance, suggests that irony's "distancing reserve," rather than just being a defense-mechanism of the ironist, may "also be interpreted as *a means to a new perspective from which things can be shown and thus seen differently.*"[29] It is in this opening up of new perspectives, in what Lear sees as the "disrupting" and "disorienting" function of irony, that irony and post-secularity cross paths. Just as the "radically antifundamentalist" post-secular position acknowledges its own historical circumstances in "articulat[ing] the avoidance of *both* the extremes of dogmatic religion and the equally dangerous hyper-rationalist convictions of the so-called secular mind," the "doubleness" of irony, can also, Hutcheon argues, "act as a way of counteracting any tendency to assume a categorical or rigid position

---

[28] See "Joseph Frank's Dostoevsky." *Consider the Lobster*. New York: Little, Brown and Company, 2006. 255-274.

[29] Hutcheon, Linda. *Irony's Edge: the theory and politics of irony*. NY: Routledge, 1995. 49. Emphasis mine.

of 'Truth' through precisely some acknowledgment of provisionality and contingency."[30] The irony in the texts I've read does not, I don't think, undermine Wallace's treatment of the "traditional" theme of religious belief, but rather, it is precisely the necessarily ambiguous and ambivalent nature of irony that enables Wallace to navigate the "radically antifundamentalist" middle position that post-secularists – and ironists – always inhabit.

---

[30] Ibid.

Exhausted Thread: A Commentary on Fiction's Progression in Thomas Pynchon, John Barth, and David Foster Wallace

Stephen Swain

Mentioning Thomas Pynchon, John Barth, David Foster Wallace, and Postmodernism in the same breath is, for all intents and purposes, old news. Seriously, it's redundant, it's been done countless times, and it's exhausted. This doesn't mean it isn't enjoyable or interesting; it's more that there appears to be very little left to discover. Many of the prominent connections have been diagnosed, dissected, and discussed to death and, for many, it seems as though all the possibilities have been exhausted. However, to point out all the textual and/or thematic similarities or to present some sort of accumulative study of these three authors (if it could be done in its entirety) would be an exhausting—yes, exhausting—endeavor. I say this as a preface to this study, mainly because I know scholars have drawn a number of similar parallels like this before, but in my research, I have yet to see these specific quotations grouped and studied together.

Hindsight, along with continued criticism and scholarship, will ultimately define this period of literature and how exactly Wallace fits into it. Accordingly, this commentary is in no way aimed at defining or claiming the shift from Modernism to Postmodernism to Post-Postmodernism, Post-Post-Postmodernism, Post-Post-#TheDeathOfFictionAndPrint or whatever genre some may propose. Instead, it is merely aimed at adding another layer of depth between three authors that are often grouped or linked together and analyzing a continuous "thread" or "line" metaphor in three specific works.

So, moving along, I want to first present three separate quotes from Pynchon, Barth, and Wallace.

In *V.* (1963), Thomas Pynchon writes:
> Conversations at the Spoon had become little more than proper nouns, literary allusions, critical or philosophical terms linked in certain ways. Depending on how you arranged the building blocks at your disposal, you were smart or stupid. Depending on how others reacted they were In or Out. The number of blocks, however, was finite.
>
> 'Mathematically, boy,' [Eigenvalue] told himself, 'if nobody else original comes along, they're bound to run out of arrangements some day. What then?' What indeed. This sort of arranging and rearranging was Decadence, but the exhaustion of all possible permutations and combinations was death. (317)

In "The Literature of Exhaustion" (1967), John Barth writes:
> By 'exhaustion' I don't mean anything so tired as the subject of physical, moral, or intellectual decadence, only the used-upness of certain forms of exhaustion of certain possibilities—by no means necessarily a cause for despair. That a great many Western artists for a great many of years have quarreled with received definitions of artistic media, genres, and forms goes without saying: pop art, dramatic and musical 'happenings,' the whole range of 'intermedia' or 'mixed-means' art, bear recentest witness to the tradition of rebelling against Tradition. (64)

Barth continues:
> [Borges'] artistic victory, if you like, is that he confronts an intellectual dead end and employs it against itself to accomplish new human work. (69-70)

Finally, in his often-cited essay "E Unibus Pluram," (1993) (which Adam Kelly has referred as part of the Interview-Essay Nexus because of its frequent use), David Foster Wallace writes:
> The next real literary 'rebels' in this country might well emerge as some weird bunch of anti-rebels, born oglers who dare somehow to back away from ironic watching, who have the childish gall actually to endorse and instantiate single-entendre principles.
>
> […]
>
> The old postmodern insurgents risked the gasp and squeal: shock,

disgust, outrage, censorship, accusations of socialism, anarchism, nihilism. Today's risks are different. The new rebels might be artists willing to risk the yawn, the rolled eyes, the cool smile, the nudged ribs, the parody of gifted ironists, the 'Oh, how banal.' To risk accusations of sentimentality, melodrama. Of overcredulity. Of willingness to be suckered by a world of lurkers and starers who fear gaze and ridicule above imprisonment without law. Who knows. Today's most engaged young fiction does seem like some kind of line's end's end. I guess that means we all get to draw our own conclusions. Have to. Are you immensely pleased. (81-82)

So, what is the connection here? Again, to emphasize the level of (self-)awareness in these authors—specifically in Wallace, who, at various instances in his life, admitted to reading the Postmodern giants is simply a wasted breath. However, it's also intriguing to imagine Pynchon, holed up in his magic bell-tower flipping through *Infinite Jest*, two bookmarks in tow, like most readers. Yet, these three quotes display a continuous intertexual "thread" or "line" reference. In fact, one can almost use the thread as a guide and follow a running commentary on the progress (or contemporary state) and purpose of high-literature. All three authors are known for a tendency toward longer works, often incorporating seemingly endless lists of digressive information, character lists that could make casting directors cringe, and narrative/formal acrobatics. The novels can easily become mazes, or labyrinths, in which hapless readers or critics are dropped, with little more than an enduring spirit and high tolerance for torture, and expected to not only understand the narrative, but also come to some conclusion about each novel and its relation to literature as a construct. It's a daunting task. Yet, in the following study, Pynchon, Barth, and Wallace appear to be leading readers along the same line or thread. In other words, each author picks up the thread left by the one before him in order to find his own way through the literary labyrinth.

Let's start with Pynchon's quote: It's almost impossible to not immediately picture the great Modernists when one reads about conversations at the Rusty Spoon consisting of "proper nouns, literary allusions, critical or philosophical terms linked in certain ways." There is an instant image of Pound and Eliot sitting in a bar (in Paris, for the active mind's sake), reading portions from "The Waste Land" and "The Cantos" to each other, while Stein and Woolf sit at a nearby table arguing over who is actually speaking.

Modernism, for all of its emphasis on originality, is essentially arranging and rearranging the various building blocks of literature—the references, allusions, languages, specific and veiled terminology, etc. There's a reason many Modernist works require a line-by-line reader companion.

Following Modernism, some literary tastes shifted to a more comfortable realistic approach. Modernism, despite its virtuosity, fell out of favor—at least in the taste of general readers (if it was ever truly considered in favor). In other words, Modernism lost its charm. Its innovative element eventually became commonplace, an expectation, the standard. Thus, as artistic movements often dictate, writers then turned from Modernism, rebelled against Modernist tastes and trends, and focused on something "new"—Realism (note Realism was not new at all [cf. Barth's discussion on Dostoevsky and Dickens]). Without going into excruciating detail, the bizarre references and allusions shifted back to the common qualities of character development and plot. Instead of rearranging the blocks with emphasis on originality or invention, writers re-rearranged the blocks back into a more honest, reliable, and (to some) less irritating art form or reflection of American life (cf. Updike in the 1960s, Carver in the 1970s/80s, amongst many others). The problem is that these shifts rarely create something new; they merely double-back to something that hasn't been chic recently. It's not necessarily invention; it's more so regurgitation.

Regardless, Pynchon notes this re-rearranging and shifting in narrative and literary form as a potentially volatile period. He writes, "if nobody else original comes along, they're bound to run out of arrangements" (317). Accordingly, Pynchon names the act, Decadence, and that, ultimately, "the exhaustion of all possible permutations and combinations was death." The two buzzwords here are Decadence and Exhaustion. The fear, in this case, is that if literature, as constituted in the mid-20th century, continued, then the arrangements would be exhausted and literature itself would "die." Perhaps "Die" here could more accurately be compared to utter stagnation. Yes, the Moderns championed originality in narrative and style (cf. Eliot's "Tradition and the Individual Talent") and the Realists campaigned for a return to emphasizing realistic characters and plot; however, like all original, genuine, sincere, innovative movements (even if they're not completely original—just merely a recycled artifact), eventually the well runs dry, the market (artistically and economically) becomes saturated, and the movement or genre "dies."

The flow and trends of artistic genres or movements is rather maze-like in that a series of artistic developments (or turns, if you will) can often lead someone back to exactly where he/she started. If artists are merely making left and right turns, they'll never go down far enough to reach the Minotaur. Eventually, genres suffer death and exhaustion. It's up to the artist to continuously reinvent genres, to create some new approach. However, in terms of literature, there is a continuous thread for most serious writers. In the face of exhaustion, the artist must continue to follow his/her thread. Or risk becoming stale or stagnant.

If in *V.* Pynchon forecasts death in 1963, Barth confirms its passing in 1967 with "The Literature of Exhaustion." Yet, he offers some glimmer of re-birth. First, I'd like to point out the obvious connection here. The essay's title, "The Literature of Exhaustion," appears to pick up directly on Pynchon's line of thinking in this specific excerpt of *V.* Granted, the concept of exhaustion in literature, at that time, could be applied across the spectrum. However, it fits too nicely to be ignored, both in Pynchon and Barth's style and (anxiety of) influence and mere chorological proximity. Similar to Pynchon's critique, Barth explains, "By 'exhaustion' I don't mean anything so tired as the subject of physical, moral, or intellectual decadence, only the used-upness of certain forms or exhaustion of certain possibilities" (64). Conveniently, the word "decadence" is used here as well. Clearly, Barth is not challenging the content of most writers, but more so the formal conventions used in telling narratives. Life consists of "physical, moral, and intellectual decadence"; it's nearly impossible for a writer to coherently *NOT* write about these aspects. The issue then, as it becomes clear, is that the form has become tired. Even the most innovative technique or approach seems trite or contrived. Writers can only arrange and rearrange the boxes a finite number of times; or else, it becomes, Pynchon notes, "technique for the sake of technique—Catatonic Expressionism" (317). Barth notes numerous examples of this, like the "unbound, unpaginated, randomly assembled novel-in-a-box and the desirability of printing *Finnegans Wake* on a very long roller-towel" (65). Like Pynchon, Barth questions literature's next move or contemplates its next turn in the maze.

However, unlike Pynchon's paranoid pessimism, Barth offers a silver, though bleak, lining referring to Jorge Luis Borges. For brevity's sake, it is only important to observe that Barth commends Borges for "confront[ing] an intellectual dead end and employ[ing] it against itself to accomplish new human work" (69-70). Suffice it to say, Barth sees possibility in innovation and invention in the future. However, a writer must confront (Pynchon's) dead end and turn it on itself in order to create something new. The continuous thread, as Barth references, does offer some possibility.

And finally we arrive at Wallace. It's no secret that Wallace honed his early skills on the Postmoderns. Any research of the Wallace canon will produce numerous references to Pynchon and Barth. However, it's also no secret that Wallace attempted to push past the boundaries of Postmodernism. His first novel, *The Broom of the System*, plays right into the Postmodern aesthetic; however, his short story, "Westward the Course of Empire Takes Its Way," attempts, as he describes in the other half of the Interview-Essay Nexus, to "get to the Armageddon-explosion, the goal metafiction's always been about, I wanted to get it over with, and then out of the rubble reaffirm the idea of art being a living transaction between humans, whether the transaction was erotic or altruistic, or sadistic" (142, cf. "An Interview with David Foster Wallace"). In destroying the genre, imploding its convention, Wallace seeks to offer some "new" or "sincerely innovative" art—some connection to the reader/viewer that doesn't appear like a narrative or literary device.

Returning back to quote from "E Unibus Pluram," it's clear that the literary purpose here, whether Wallace intended direct association or not, responds to both Pynchon and Barth. Pynchon forecasted "death," Barth acknowledged "death," and Wallace describes a possible rebirth—though very different from Barth's. Whereas Barth championed for invention, some formal push beyond the death of literature, Wallace more accurately defines (or tries to define) what the push could look like. Perhaps Wallace's own work adhered to this definition. There's plenty of skeptical criticism concerning the sincerity and/or irony in Wallace's narrative voice—especially, his apparent emphasis on awareness and compassion, most notably in his later works. However, this excerpt, in its own way, does respond to the quotes from both Pynchon and Barth, because, ultimately, the Postmodern aesthetic finally became a standard convention or joke in and of itself. Wallace tried to turn joke back on itself. He used or pushed past the dead end in order to jump-start fiction, to give it some sort of pulse. (cf. "Fiction's about what it is to be a fucking human being" [131, "An

Interview"]). He followed the thread, escaped the maze, and, by doing so, knocked the walls of the maze down.

It's imperative to note that the buzzwords (decadence and exhaustion) do not show up in Wallace's excerpt. The specific words don't; however, Wallace notes, "The new rebels might be artists willing to risk the yawn, the rolled eyes, the cool smile, the nudged ribs, the parody of gifted ironists, the 'Oh, how banal'" (81). If this isn't exhaustion, then it's certainly collective malaise. Irony, as it became for Wallace, as many scholars have noted, was both a symptom and diagnosis of this exhaustion. If all current narrative forms are exhausted, then the whole thing needs to implode. The Armageddon, as Wallace noted, should ideally generate something "new"—and if not new, then at least fresh, honest, impassioned, disturbing, or hysterical. Something. There's an encouraged awareness in writing. For all the narrative forms and literary devices, literature (and literary history) is ripe with the possibilities of exhaustion. Perhaps it is important to note Barth's statement that an artist "need only be aware of their existence or possibility, acknowledge them, and with the aid of very special gifts [...] go straight through the maze to the accomplishment of his work" (75-6).

It seems too perfect that if Pynchon described the artist as fearing death in the finite maze of literary exhaustion and Barth described the artist as Theseus in the middle of the labyrinth holding his thread, trying to find his way out, then it's only fitting that Wallace, in 1993, describes literature at "some kind of line's end's end" (82).

Works Cited

Barth, John. "Literature of Exhaustion." *The Friday Book: Essays and Other Non-Fiction*. Baltimore: John Hopkins U. P. 1984. 64-76.

Pynchon, Thomas. *V.* New York: Harper Collins.

Wallace, David Foster. "An Interview with David Foster Wallace." *The Review of Contemporary Fiction* 31.2 (Summer 1993): 127-150. Print.

—. "E Unibus Pluram." *A Supposedly Fun Thing I'll Never Do Again*. New York: BackBay Books. 1997. 21-83.

Bios

Diego Báez grew up in Normal, Illinois and graduated with an MFA in Creative Writing from Rutgers University Newark. An inaugural fellow at CantoMundo in 2010, his poetry, fiction, and reviews have appeared most recently at *Ostrich Review*, the *Acentos Review*, and the *Los Angeles Review of Books*. He lives in Chicago and teaches at the City Colleges.

Ryan M. Blanck is a high school English teacher and writer, having written and self-published six books, including *Supposedly Fun Things*, a collection of narrative and critical essays inspired by the creative nonfiction of David Foster Wallace. Ryan presented his paper, "What the Hell is Water?" at the Work in Process conference at the University of Antwerp. His current project is titled "Infinite Legos," a recreation of scenes from *Infinite Jest* in Lego sculptures.

Emily Brutton is a senior English Studies and Theatre Education double major at Illinois State University. Throughout the last two semesters, she has been interning for the David Foster Wallace Conference. Her efforts have included the reformatting of the *DFW Memorial Book*, the editing of the anthology of works from last year's conference, and organizing the Oral Interpretation program, as well as various advertising and social media projects. She is currently working on an undergraduate thesis concerning *Hamlet* and *Infinite Jest*.

Matt Bucher is a writer and editor living in Austin, Texas. He is the editorial director of Sideshow Media Group Press. Since 2002 he has served as administrator of the David Foster Wallace listserv, *wallace-l*.

Jeffrey Calzaloia is a novelist whose ambitious work may not achieve commercial success but whose investment in producing high-quality literary fiction remains strong. Inspired by novelists such as John Crowley, Toni Morrison, Gene Wolfe, Cormac McCarthy, Junot Díaz, Samuel R. Delany, Marcel Proust, and (of course) David Foster Wallace, as well as poets such as Gerard Manley Hopkins, Wallace Stevens, Leonie Adams, and John Brooks Wheelwright, Mr. Calzaloia is a fresh young talent to watch out for in the years to come.

Jane L. Carman is the founder of Lit Fest Press, *Festival Writer*, and the reading series a reading eXperiment and Festival of Language. She holds a PhD from Illinois State University where she is a former Sutherland Fellow. Her interests include the theory, pedagogy, creation, publication, and dissemination of contemporary American literature, especially that which moves the canon and art forward. Her book, *Tangled in Motion*, was published by Journal of Experimental Fiction Books in 2015 and is a genre-less experiment in form and content. Her critical and creative work can be found in *American Book Review*, *elimae*, *Palooka*, *Dirty : Dirty* (Jaded Ibis Productions), *580-Split*, *JAC*, *Devil's Lake*, and many others.

Amy L. Eggert teaches composition, literature, and creative writing for Bradley University and Midstate College in Peoria, Illinois. She has a PhD in English Studies from Illinois State University with a specialization in trauma theory and creative writing. She is the author of *Scattershot: Collected Fictions* (2015) from Lit Fest Press, and her work appears in *Festival Writer*, *Bluffs Literary Magazine*, *Heart*, *American Book Review*, and in several university literary journals.

Danielle S. Ely first read *Infinite Jest* in a six week summer immersion course at The College of Saint Rose in 2009. She went on to complete a Master's Thesis about it in 2011. She has presented instantiations of her thesis at conferences like Sex…or Something Like It, Multiplicities: Mapping Identity Through Literature, and last year's David Foster Wallace Conference. She's an adjunct instructor at Columbia-Greene Community College, Hudson Valley Community College, and Dutchess Community College.

Christine Harkin is an independent scholar whose academic writing focuses on feminism, Modernism, and popular culture. She acts as a writing, editing, and brand naming consultant to corporations large and small and is writing two novels. Christine, who earned her BA from UC Berkeley and her MA from California State University is still debating further graduate studies in literature.

Jeff Jarot is a writer who teaches in Plainfield Consolidated School District 202. He holds a BA in English from Illinois Wesleyan University, a BA in English Education from Illinois State University, an MA in English with an emphasis in literature and film from Northern Illinois University, and an MA in creative writing from Illinois State University in December 2013. He presented both his fiction and critical work at the David Foster Wallace Conference held at Illinois State University in May of 2014, and his fiction has appeared in *Festival Writer*. Mr. Jarot lives in Plainfield, Illinois with his wife and three children.

Carissa Kampmeier earned a Master's degree in English Studies from Illinois State University and will be starting work on a doctoral degree in contemporary literature at Florida State University this fall. Her research interests include the ways that contemporary American fiction is both reacting to and influenced by the postmodern movement, the genre of the mixtape as a form of lifewriting, and the critical analysis of horror films.

Ashlie M. Kontos is a master's student of English at the University of Texas at Tyler. Her research interests include shame in literature; literary theory—specifically metamodernism; post-Holocaust Jewish literature; and the literature and philosophy of David Foster Wallace. She has her BA in English with minors in history and classical studies. Her essay titled "Nomina Nuda Tenemus: Jonathan Safran Foer Finding Meaning Within Empty Names, or (re)Construction of Deconstruction" won the University of Louisiana at Lafayette's Darrell Bourque Award (2012) and was published in *Media, Technology and the Imagination* in 2013 by Cambridge Scholars Publishing.

Daniel Leonard is an MFA candidate in poetry at Boston University. He earned a master's degree in philosophy at Katholieke Universiteit Leuven in Belgium and a bachelor's degree in interdisciplinary studies at Wheaton College in Illinois. He was chosen by Robert Pinsky as First Runner-Up in the 2014 Tennessee Williams/New Orleans Literary Festival Poetry Contest. He is also the creator of *3eanuts*, a humor website reviewed online by *TIME*, *Entertainment Weekly*, *Washington Post*, and others.

Francesco Levato is a poet, translator, and new media artist. Recent books include *Endless, Beautiful, Exact*; *Elegy for Dead Languages*; *War Rug*; and *Creaturing* (as translator). He has collaborated and performed with various composers, including Philip Glass, and his cinépoetry has been exhibited in galleries and featured at film festivals in Berlin, Chicago, New York, and elsewhere. He founded the Chicago School of Poetics, holds an MFA in poetry, and is working on his PhD in English Studies.

Christopher Michaelson is associate professor of ethics and business law at the University of St. Thomas, Opus College of Business and is also on the Business and Society faculty of New York University's Stern School of Business. His research uses the arts and humanities to explore meaningful work, global ethics, and emerging risks. Christopher's PhD in philosophy is from the University of Minnesota, specializing in ethics and aesthetics.

Mike Miley teaches literature and film studies at Metairie Park Country Day School. His work has appeared in *Bright Lights Film Journal*, *Film International*, *Moving Image Source*, *Music and the Moving Image*, and the *New Orleans Review*.

Shannon Minifie is a PhD candidate in the English department at Queen's University in Kingston, Ontario. She received her Honours BA from the University of Toronto, and her MA from Clark University (Worcester, Massachusetts). Between those degrees, she worked in publishing at the famed small press, Coach House Books, in Toronto. She studies and teaches 19th-21st century American literature, and is currently writing a dissertation on David Foster Wallace and the context of post-secularism.

JoAnna Novak is a writer of fiction, nonfiction, and poetry. She lives in Massachusetts.

Robert Ryan holds a Master's degree in English from Binghamton University and is the Editor-in-Chief of *Wreck Park: A Journal of Interesting Fictions, Interested Criticism*. He lives in upstate New York.

Mark Sheridan is a graduate student in the Department of English at the University of Texas at Austin. He specializes in American literature, with a focus on late-twentieth-century experimental fiction and metafiction.

Stephen Swain graduated from Millikin University with a BA in secondary English education in 2009. He completed his MA in English literature at DePaul University in Chicago. He is currently a professor of English at DePaul University and Truman College in Chicago. In his independent research, Swain studies postmodern and contemporary American fiction, specifically the work of David Foster Wallace.

Z. Bart Thornton—who teaches English and serves as Dean of Faculty at The Collegiate School in Richmond, Virginia—holds a PhD from The University of Texas, where he wrote his dissertation on Don DeLillo and Deconstructivist architectural aesthetics. He has published fiction and criticism in the *Minnesota Review*, *PMLA*, *Mosaic*, and *Texas Monthly*. He is currently working on a book-length study of dissolute intellectuals in American fiction and European film.

www.ingramcontent.com/pod-product-compliance
Lightning Source LLC
Chambersburg PA
CBHW050801160426
43192CB00010B/1603